BEST-EVER COOK'S COLLECTION

PASTA

BEST-EVER COOK'S COLLECTION

PASTA

THE DEFINITIVE COOK'S COLLECTION:
200 STEP-BY-STEP PASTA RECIPES

Consultant Editor:
Linda Fraser

PARRAGON

First published in 1996 by Ultimate Editions
an imprint of Anness Publishing Limited
Hermes House, 88-89 Blackfriars Road, London SE1 8HA

© 1996 Anness Publishing Limited

This edition published in 1997 by
Parragon
Units 13-17 Avonbridge Trading Estate,
Atlantic Road, Avonmouth, Bristol BS11 9QD

ISBN 0-75252-333-3 paperback
ISBN 0-75252-354-6 hardback

A CIP catalogue record for this book is available from the British Library

Publisher: Joanna Lorenz
Senior Cookery Editor: Linda Fraser
Cookery Editor: Rosemary Wilkinson
Copy Editor: Val Barrett
Designer: Bill Mason
Recipes: Catherine Atkinson, Carla Capalbo, Maxine Clark, Roz Denny,
Christine France, Sarah Gates, Shirley Gill, Norma MacMillan, Sue Maggs,
Elizabeth Martin, Annie Nichols, Jenny Stacy, Liz Trigg, Laura Washburn, Steven Wheeler
Photographs: Karl Adamson, Edward Allwright, David Armstrong, Steve Baxter,
Jo Brewer, James Duncan, Michelle Garrett, Amanda Heywood, Patrick McLeavey, Michael Michaels
Stylists: Madeleine Brehaut, Jo Brewer, Carla Capalbo, Michelle Garrett, Hilary Guy, Amanda Heywood,
Patrick McLeavey, Blake Minton, Kirsty Rawlings, Elizabeth Wolf-Cohen
Food for Photography: Wendy Lee, Lucy McElvie, Jane Stevenson, Elizabeth Wolf-Cohen
Illustrator: Anna Koska

Printed and bound in Italy

1 3 5 7 9 10 8 6 4 2

Notes
For all recipes, quantities are given in both metric and imperial measures and, where appropriate, measures are also
given in standard cups and spoons. Follow one set, but not a mixture because they are not interchangeable.

Standard spoon and cup measurements are level.
1 tbsp = 15ml, 1 tsp = 5ml, 1 cup = 250ml/8fl oz

Australian standard tablespoons are 20ml. Australian readers should use 3 tsp in place of 1 tbsp for measuring small
quantities of gelatine, cornflour, salt etc.

Size 3 (medium) eggs should be used unless otherwise stated.

CONTENTS

Introduction

PASTA HAS RAPIDLY become one of Western society's staple foods, travelling across the world in various forms from Asia and South America. Its origins are unclear, but a type of pasta was certainly made in Sicily, the "grain store" of Rome, in the days of the Roman Empire. It has also existed in China and Japan for many centuries, but in very different forms and shapes.

The enormous popularity of pasta is due to its incredible versatility, and its value for money. Pasta can stretch a few store-cupboard ingredients to make a satisfying meal fit for a king! You can produce sauces with small amounts of meat, mix them with pasta and produce a filling and nutritious dish. Most wheat-flour-and-water (commercial dried) pasta contains more proteins and carbohydrates than potatoes, so when combined with a sauce of vegetables, cheese or meat, it gives a good nutritional balance. It is a fine source of energy too – better than sugar, as it releases energy at a slower prolonged rate, and will give you a lift if you are tired and hungry. Pasta is only fattening if eaten in over-large quantities with too much sauce! Italians fill up on the pasta itself, the sauce being an adornment to enhance the flavour.

Pasta is very easy to make at home if you have patience and a little time to spare. The result is exciting and delicious, even if it is a little soggy to begin with! It's a little like making bread: once you have mastered the technique, you can make one of life's staples.

The recipes in this book are mostly based on a family of four people, but they can be easily halved for two or doubled for eight. There are chapters on soups, fish and seafood, salads and starters and sauces, as well as suggestions, meals in minutes, midweek meals, quick and easy dishes and simple suppers to provide you with a best-ever pasta meal for every occasion.

Pasta Types

When buying dried pasta, choose good-quality well-known brands. Of the "fresh" pasta sold in sealed packs in super-markets, the filled or stuffed varieties are worth buying; noodles and ribbon pasta are better bought dried, as these tend to have more bite when cooked. However, if you are lucky enough to live near an Italian delicatessen where pasta is made on the premises, it will usually be of very good quality. Fresh is not necessarily better, but the final choice is yours – the best pasta is home-made, as then you can be sure of the quality of the ingredients used and also of the finished texture.

You will see from this book that the sauces are almost limitless in their variety, as are the pasta shapes themselves. There are no hard-and-fast rules regarding which shape to use with which pasta sauce: it's really a matter of personal preference. However, there are a few guidelines to follow, such as that thin spaghetti suits seafood sauces, thicker spaghetti is good with creamy sauces (as in, for instance, Spaghetti alla Carbonara) and thick tubular pasta, like rigatoni, penne and so on, suits rustic sauces full of bits that will be caught in the pasta itself.

vermicelli

macaroni

quick-cook macaroni

fresh cuttlefish-ink tagliatelle

tagliatelle: tomato, spinach and plain

orzo or puntalette

small soup pasta

fresh caramellone

fresh ravioli

fresh cappelletti

fresh paglia e fieno ('straw and hay' tagliarini)

fresh tortellini

fresh pappardelle

fresh beetroot
tagliatelle

wholemeal spaghetti

tomato
spaghetti

spinach
spaghetti

pipe rigate

fresh wild-mushroom
tagliatelle

conchigliette

campanelle

farfalle (pasta bows)

cannelloni

fettuccia riccia

unghe

spirali

rigatoni

pasta shells (conchiglie)

lasagne

spinach lasagne

garganelle

wholemeal shells

orecchiette

Sauces and Pastes

There is an infinite variety of ready-made sauces and pastes available which you can add to your own sauce to make it richer or to deepen the flavour. Some can even be incorporated into pasta dough: for example, you can make mushroom or tomato or even pesto pasta.

Anchovies: salted Whole anchovies preserved in salt need to be rinsed and the backbone removed before use. They have a fresher flavour than canned anchovy fillets in oil. Used in moderation, anchovies add a fishy depth to sauces and soups.

Capers These are little green flower buds preserved in vinegar or salt. They add a sharp piquancy to rich sauces and are particularly good with tomatoes and many cheeses.

Carbonara sauce Although your own version made from the recipe in this book will be much better, ready-made carbonara sauce is a useful standby for a quick meal – add sautéed fresh mushrooms or more bacon to make it go further.

Garlic: chopped A great time-saver, eliminating the need for peeling and chopping. Use it straight out of the jar.

Mushroom paste A delicacy available from Italian delicatessens. Add a generous spoonful to freshly cooked pasta with a little cream for a quick sauce, or incorporate into dough to make delicious mushroom pasta.

Olive paste Cuts out all that stoning and chopping. Delicious stirred into hot pasta with chopped fresh tomato or added by the spoonful to enrich a tomato or meat sauce.

Pesto The commercial version of fresh basil pesto. Brands vary, but it is a very useful store-cupboard standby to stir into hot pasta and soups.

Pesto: fresh Some supermarkets produce their own "fresh" pesto, sold in tubs in the chilled cabinet. This is infinitely superior to the bottled variety, although your own freshly made pesto will be even better.

Pesto: red A commercial sauce made from tomatoes and red peppers to stir into hot pasta or to pep up soups.

Tomato pasta sauce Again, a good standby or base for a quick meal. Vary by adding chopped anchovies and olives, or pour over freshly cooked stuffed pasta such as tortellini.

Tomato purée An essential if you are making a sauce from insipid fresh tomatoes. It will intensify any tomato-based sauce and will help thicken meat sauces. It will also make tomato pasta if added to the basic dough ingredients.

Tomatoes: canned plum No store-cupboard should be without these – invaluable for making any tomato sauce or stew when good fresh tomatoes are not readily available.

Tomatoes: canned chopped Usually made from Italian plum tomatoes which have a fuller flavour than most, these are the heart of a good tomato sauce if you cannot find really ripe, red, tasty, fresh tomatoes.

Tomatoes: passata A useful store-cupboard ingredient, this is pulped tomato that has been strained to remove the seeds. It makes a good base for a tomato sauce, though chopped canned tomatoes can also be used.

Tomatoes: sun-dried in oil These tomatoes are drained and chopped and added to tomato-based dishes to give a deeper, almost roasted tomato flavour.

Below, clockwise from top left: Salted anchovies; canned chopped tomatoes; pesto; olive paste; canned plum tomatoes; tomato purée; passata.

Eastern Pasta

Various forms of noodle or pasta exist outside Europe and America. They are found mainly in China and Japan, but also throughout Malaysia, Hong Kong and the rest of the Far East, including parts of India and Tibet.

This pasta, usually in noodle form and often enhanced with a sprinkling of vegetables or fish, adds variety to the sometimes monotonous staple diet of rice and beans eaten by the poorer sections of the population. Some types of pasta are used to give bulk to soups; others are eaten as a filling dish to stave off hunger during the day. They are made from the staple crops of each region – whether rice flour, soya bean flour or potato flour – and are cooked in different ways: some are soaked and then fried, some are boiled and fried and some are rolled out and stuffed like ravioli, but most are simply boiled. Some turn transparent when cooked.

Oriental egg noodles are usually made with wheat flour and can be treated in the same way as ordinary Western pasta. Buckwheat and fresh wholemeal noodles are cooked in a similar fashion. Fresh white noodles do not contain egg but are cooked in the same way as egg noodles. Some dried egg noodles come in discs or blocks and are "cooked" by immersion in boiling water in which they are then left to soak for a few minutes. As with Western pasta, oriental noodles can be flavoured with additional

ingredients such as prawns, carrot and spinach.

Won ton skins, like thin squares of rolled-out pasta, are used for stuffing and making different filled shapes. Although oriental pasta is available in a variety of long noodle types, it doesn't seem to be made into the shapes we are used to seeing in Europe and America: you will often find it wound into balls and beautifully packaged.

Above: Eastern noodles include (from top left, clockwise) oriental rice flour noodles, rice vermicelli, rice stick noodles, handmade amoy flour vermicelli, medium egg noodles, fresh brown mein, egg noodles, rice stick vermicelli, fresh thin egg noodles, Japanese wheat flour noodles, Ho Fan vermicelli, spinach vegetable noodles, carrot vegetable noodles, won ton skins, wheat flour noodles, fresh white mein, buckwheat noodles, shrimp egg noodles.

Equipment

To make pasta, a bare minimum of equipment is needed – practised hands would say that only a clean work surface and a rolling pin were strictly necessary. However, there are several gadgets to assist the pasta maker.

Bowls A set of bowls is useful for mixing, whisking and so on.

Chopping board A hygienic nylon board is recommended for cutting and chopping.

Colander A large colander is essential for draining cooked pasta quickly.

Cook's knife A large all-purpose cook's knife is necesary for cutting pasta and for chopping.

Flour dredger This is useful for dusting pasta with small amounts of flour.

Large metal spoon For folding in and serving sauces.

Measuring spoons For accurately measuring small quantities of ingredients for pasta.

Pasta machine or roller Vital for kneading, rolling and cutting pasta – a real labour-saver. Attachments for other shapes are available.

Pasta or pastry wheel For cutting pasta with a decorated edge, such as pasta bows.

Pastry brush For removing excess flour from pasta and for brushing pasta with water, milk or beaten egg to seal.

Pestle and mortar For hand-grinding pesto and crushing black peppercorns.

Ravioli cutter For cutting or stamping out individual raviolis; can be round or square. A selection of pastry cutters will serve the same purpose.

Ravioli tray (raviolatore) For making sheets of ravioli quickly and neatly – with practice.

Rolling pin Pasta pins are available in specialist shops. These are long, thin and tapered at each end, but you have to be quite adept to use them. An ordinary heavy wooden rolling pin will do instead.

Slotted spoon Useful for draining small amounts of food.

Small grater For grating nutmeg and Parmesan cheese

Vegetable knife For preparing vegetables and paring lemons, and for delicate work.

Vegetable peeler For shaving Parmesan cheese, and chocolate for sweet pasta.

Whisk Essential for beating eggs thoroughly and combining sauces smoothly.

bowls

pasta machine

flour dredger

slotted spoon

pestle and mortar

cutters

rolling pin

large metal spoon

colander

cook's knife

vegetable knife

small grater

vegetable peeler

pastry brush

pastry wheel

ravioli tray
(raviolatore)

measuring spoons

metal whisk

ravioli cutter

About Pasta

Most pasta is made from durum wheat flour and water – durum is a special kind of wheat with a very high protein content. Egg pasta, *pasta all'uova*, contains flour and eggs, and is used for flat pasta such as tagliatelle, or for lasagne. Very little wholemeal pasta is eaten in Italy, but it is quite popular in other countries.

All these types of pasta are available dried in packets and will keep almost indefinitely. Fresh pasta is now widely available and can be bought in most good supermarkets. It can be very good, but can never compare to home-made egg pasta.

Pasta comes in countless shapes and sizes. It is very difficult to give a definitive list, as the names for the shapes vary from country to country. In some cases, just within Italy, the same shape can appear with several different names, depending upon which region it is in. The pasta shapes called for in this book, as well as many others, are illustrated in the introduction. The most common names have been listed there.

Most of the recipes in this book specify the pasta shape most appropriate for a particular sauce. They can, of course, be replaced with another kind. A general rule is that long pasta goes better with tomato or thinner sauces, while short pasta is best for chunkier, meatier sauces. But this rule should not be followed too rigidly. Part of the fun of cooking and eating pasta is in the endless possible combinations of sauce and pasta shapes.

How to Make Egg Pasta by Hand

This classic recipe for egg pasta from Emilia Romagna region, around Bolognia, calls for just three ingredients; flour, eggs and a little salt. In other regions of Italy water, milk or oil are sometimes added. Use plain or strong white flour, and large eggs. As a general guide, use 50g/2oz/½ cup of flour to each egg. Quantities will vary with the exact size of the eggs.

To serve 3–4
150g/5oz/1¼ cups flour
2 eggs
pinch of salt

To serve 4–6
210g/7½oz/scant 2
   cups flour
3 eggs
pinch of salt

To serve 6–8
275g/10oz/2½ cups flour
4 eggs
pinch of salt

1 Place the flour in the centre of a clean, smooth work surface. Make a well in the middle. Break the eggs into the well. Add a pinch of salt.

2 Start beating the eggs with a fork, gradually drawing the flour from the inside walls of the well. As the pasta thickens, continue the mixing with your hands. Incorporate as much flour as possible until the mixture forms a mass. It will still be lumpy. If it still sticks to your hands, add a little more flour. Set the dough aside. Scrape off all traces of the dough from the work surface until it is perfectly smooth. Wash and dry your hands.

3 Lightly flour the work surface. Knead the dough by pressing it away from you with the heel of your hands, and then folding it over towards you. Repeat this action over and over, turning the dough as you knead. Work for about 10 minutes, or until the dough is smooth and elastic.

4 If you are using more than two eggs, divide the dough in half. Flour the rolling pin and the work surface. Pat the dough into a disc and begin rolling it out into a flat circle, rotating it a quarter turn after each roll to keep its shape round. Roll until the disc is about 3mm/⅛in thick.

time to keep it evenly thin. By the end (this process should not last more than 8 to 10 minutes or the dough will lose its elasticity) the whole sheet should be smooth and almost transparent. If the dough is still sticky, lightly flour your hands as you continue rolling and stretching it in the same way.

8 To cut tagliatelle, fettuccine or tagliolini, fold the sheet of pasta into a flat roll about 10cm/4in wide. Cut across the roll to form noodles of the desired width. Tagliolini is 3mm/⅛in; fettuccine is 4mm/⅙in; tagliatelle is 5mm/¼in. After cutting, open out the noodles and let them dry for about 5 minutes before cooking. These noodles may be stored for some weeks without refrigeration. Allow the noodles to dry completely before storing them, uncovered, in a dry cupboard, and use as required.

5 Roll out the dough until it is paper-thin by rolling up on to the rolling pin and simultaneously giving a sideways stretch with your hands. Wrap the near edge of the dough around the centre of the rolling pin and begin rolling the dough up away from you. As you roll back and forth, slide your hands from the centre towards the outer edges of the pin, stretching and thinning out the pasta.

7 If you are making pasta noodles, such as tagliatelle, fettuccine, etc, lay a clean dish towel on a table or other flat surface, and unroll the pasta sheet onto it, letting about one-third of the sheet hang over the edge of the table. Rotate the dough about every 10 minutes. Roll out the second sheet of dough if you are using more than two eggs. After 25–30 minutes the pasta will have dried enough to cut. Do not allow to overdry or the pasta will crack as it is cut.

6 Quickly repeat these movements until about two-thirds of the sheet of pasta is wrapped around the pin. Lift and turn the wrapped pasta sheet about 45° before unrolling it. Repeat the rolling and stretch process, starting from a new point of the sheet each

9 To cut the pasta for lasagne or pappardelle, do not fold or dry the rolled-out dough. Lasagne is made from rectangles approximately 13 × 9cm/5 × 3½in. Pappardelle are large noodles cut with a fluted pasta or pastry wheel. They are about 2cm/¾in wide.

Egg Pasta Made by Machine

Making pasta with a machine is quick and easy. The results are perhaps not quite as fine as with handmade pasta, but they are certainly better than ready-made pastas will ever be.

You will need a pasta-making machine, either hand-cranked or electric. Use the same proportions of eggs, flour and salt as for Handmade Egg Pasta.

1 Place the flour in the centre of a clean smooth work surface. Make a well in the middle. Break the eggs into the well. Add a pinch of salt. Start beating the eggs with a fork, gradually drawing the flour from the inside walls of the well. As the paste thickens, continue mixing with your hands. Incorporate as much flour as possible until the mixture forms a mass. It will still be lumpy. If it sticks to your hands, add a little more flour. Set the dough aside and scrape the work surface clean.

2 Set the machine rollers at their widest (kneading) setting. Pull off a piece of dough the size of a small orange. Place the remaining dough between two soup plates. Feed the dough through the rollers. Fold it in half, end to end, and feed it through again about 7–8 times, turning it and folding it over after each kneading. The dough should be smooth and fairly evenly rectangular. If it sticks to the machine, brush with flour. Lay it out on a lightly floured work surface or on a clean dish towel, and repeat with the remaining dough, broken into pieces roughly the same size.

3 Adjust the machine to the next line setting. Feed each strip through once only, and replace on the drying surface. Keep them in the order in which they were first kneaded.

4 Reset the machine to the next setting. Repeat, passing each strip through once. Repeat for each remaining roller setting until the pasta is the right thickness – for most purposes this is given by the next to last setting, except for very delicate strips such as tagliolini, or for ravioli. If the pasta strips get too long, cut them in half to allow for easier handling.

5 Be sure the pasta is fairly dry, but not brittle, or the noodles may stick together when cut. Select the desired width of cutter, and feed the strips through.

6 Separate the noodles, and leave to dry for at least 15 minutes before using. They may be stored for some weeks without refrigeration. Allow them to dry completely before storing them, uncovered, in a dry cupboard. They may also be frozen, first loose on trays and then packed together.

7 If you are making stuffed pasta, such as ravioli, cannelloni, etc, do not let the pasta strips dry out before filling them, but proceed immediately with the individual recipe of your choice.

GREEN PASTA

Follow the same recipe, adding 50g/2oz/¼ cup cooked, very finely chopped, spinach (which has been squeezed very dry) to the eggs and flour. You may have to add a little more flour to absorb the moisture from the spinach. This pasta is very suitable for stuffed recipes, as it seals better than plain egg pasta.

How to Cook Dried Pasta

Ready-made and homemade pasta are cooked in the same way, though the timings vary greatly. Home-made pasta cooks virtually in the time it takes for the water to return to the boil after it is put in the pan.

1 Always cook pasta in a large amount of rapidly boiling water. Use at least 1–2 litres/ 1¾-3½ pints/4-8 cups water to each 115g/4oz pasta.

2 The water should be salted at least 2 minutes before the pasta is added, to give the salt time to dissolve. Add 25ml/1½ tbsp salt per 450g/1lb pasta. You may want to vary the saltiness of the cooking water.

3 Drop the pasta into the boiling water all at once. Use a wooden spoon to help ease long pasta in as it softens, to prevent it from breaking. Stir frequently to prevent the pasta sticking together or to the pan. Cook the pasta at a fast boil, but be prepared to lower the heat if it boils over.

4 Timing is critical in pasta cooking. Follow the instructions on the packet for ready-made pasta, but it is best in all cases to test for readiness by tasting. In Italy pasta is always eaten *al dente*, which means firm to the bite. Cooked this way it is just tender, but its "soul" (the innermost part) is still firm. Overcooked pasta will be mushy.

5 Place a colander in the sink before the pasta has finished cooking. As soon as the pasta is done, tip it all into the colander (you may first want to reserve a cupful of the hot cooking water to add to the sauce if it needs thinning). Shake the colander lightly to remove most but not all of the cooking water. Pasta should never be over-drained.

6 Quickly turn the pasta into a warmed serving dish and immediately toss it with a little butter or oil, or the prepared sauce. Alternatively, turn it into the cooking pan with the sauce, where it will be cooked for a further 1–2 minutes as it is mixed into the sauce. Never allow pasta to sit undressed, as it will stick together and become unpalatable.

How to Cook Egg Pasta

Fresh egg pasta, especially home-made, cooks very much faster than dried pasta. Make sure everything is ready (the sauce and serving dishes) before you start boiling egg pasta, as there will not be time once the cooking starts, and egg pasta becomes soft and mushy very quickly if left too long.

1 Always cook pasta in a large amount of rapidly boiling water. Use at least 1–2 litres/ 1¾-3½ pints/4-8 cups water to a quantity of pasta made with 115g/4oz/1 cup flour. Salt the water as you would for dried pasta.

2 Drop the pasta into the boiling water all at once. Stir gently to prevent the pasta sticking together or to the pan. Cook the pasta at a fast boil.

3 Freshly made pasta can be done as little as 15 seconds after the cooking water comes back to the boil. Stuffed pasta takes a few minutes longer. When done, tip the pasta into the colander and proceed as for dried pasta.

Macaroni

Macaroni is the generic name for any hollow pasta. This method is for making garganelle.

1 Cut squares of pasta dough using a sharp knife on a floured surface.

2 Wrap the squares around a pencil or chopstick on the diagonal to form tubes. Slip off and allow to dry slightly.

SPINACH PASTA

Use 150g/5oz frozen leaf spinach, cooked and squeezed dry, a pinch of salt, 2 eggs, about 200g/7oz/1¾ cups plain white flour, or a little more if the pasta is sticky. Proceed as for Basic Pasta Dough, but liquidize the spinach with the eggs to give a fine texture.

Tagliatelle

Tagliatelle can also be made with a pasta machine, but it is fairly straightforward to make by hand.

1 Roll up the floured pasta dough like a Swiss roll.

2 Cut the roll into thin slices with a very sharp knife. Immediately unravel the slices to reveal the pasta ribbons. To make taglianni, cut the slices about 3mm/⅛in thick.

3 To make pappardelle, using a serrated pastry wheel, cut out wide ribbons from the rolled-out pastry dough.

Tortellini

Tortellini or "little twists" can be made with meat or vegetarian fillings and served with sauce or in a hearty soup.

1 Using a round biscuit cutter, stamp out rounds of pasta.

2 Pipe or spoon the chosen filling into the middle of each of the rounds.

3 Brush the edges with beaten egg and fold the round into a crescent shape, excluding all the air. Bend the two corners round to meet each other and press well to seal. Repeat with the remaining dough. Leave to dry on a floured dish towel for 30 minutes before cooking the tortellini.

SPINACH, RICOTTA AND PARMESAN FILLING FOR STUFFED PASTA

Serves 4–6

450g/1lb frozen spinach, thawed and squeezed dry
2.5ml/½ tsp grated nutmeg
5ml/1 tsp salt
ground black pepper
175g/6oz/¾ cup fresh ricotta or curd cheese
25g/1oz/¼ cup freshly grated Parmesan cheese

Place all the ingredients in a blender or food processor and process until smooth. Use as required in your recipe.

Ravioli

Although ravioli can be bought ready made, the very best is made at home. Serve with sauce or in a soup.

1 Cut the dough in half and wrap one portion in clear film. Roll out the pasta thinly to a rectangle on a lightly floured surface. Cover with a clean, damp dish towel and repeat with the remaining pasta. Pipe small

mounds (about 5ml/1 tsp) of filling in even rows, spacing them at 4cm/1½in intervals, across one piece of the dough. Brush the spaces between the filling with egg.

2 Using a rolling pin, lift the second sheet of pasta over the dough with the filling. Press down firmly between the pockets of filling, pushing out any air.

3 Cut into squares with a serrated ravioli cutter or sharp knife. Transfer to a floured dish towel and rest for 1 hour before cooking the ravioli.

SOUPS WITH PASTA

Pasta, Bean and Vegetable Soup

This colourful, filling soup will satisfy the largest appetite.

INGREDIENTS

Serves 4–6

115g/4oz dried borlotti or black-eyed beans, soaked overnight and drained

1.2 litres/2 pints/5 cups vegetable, poultry or meat stock

1 large onion, chopped

1 large garlic clove, finely chopped

2 celery sticks, chopped

½ red pepper, seeded and chopped

350g/12oz tomatoes, skinned, seeded and chopped or canned chopped tomatoes

225g/8oz smoked bacon loin

75g/3oz tiny soup pasta

2 courgettes, halved lengthways and sliced

15ml/1 tbsp tomato purée

salt and ground black pepper

shredded fresh basil, to garnish

1 Put the beans in a large pan. Cover with fresh cold water and bring to the boil. Boil for 10 minutes, then drain and rinse. Return the beans to the pan, add the stock and bring to the boil. Skim off the scum.

2 Add the onion, garlic, celery, red pepper, tomatoes and bacon. Bring back to the boil.

3 Cover and simmer over a low heat for 1½ hours or until the beans are just tender. Lift out the bacon. Shred the meat coarsely with two forks and set aside.

4 Add the pasta, courgettes and tomato purée to the soup. Season to taste with salt and pepper. Simmer uncovered, for a further 5–8 minutes, stirring the soup occasionally. (Check the pasta cooking time on the packet.)

5 Stir in the shredded bacon. Taste and adjust the seasoning if necessary, then serve the soup hot, sprinkled with shredded fresh basil as a garnish.

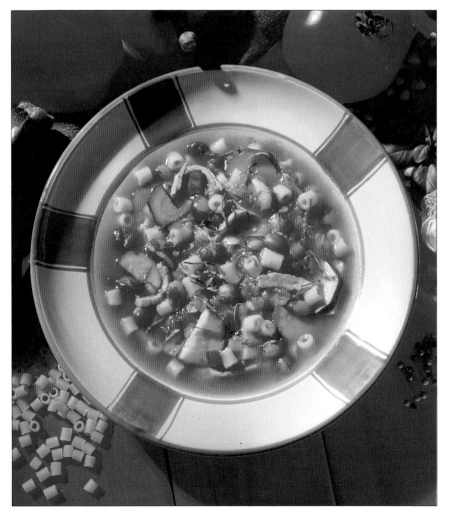

Chunky Pasta Soup

Serve this filling main-meal soup with tasty, pesto-topped French bread croûtons.

INGREDIENTS

Serves 4

115g/4oz/⅔ cup dry beans (a mixture of
    red kidney and haricot beans), soaked
    in cold water overnight
15ml/1 tbsp oil
1 onion, chopped
2 celery sticks, thinly sliced
2–3 garlic cloves, crushed
2 leeks, thinly sliced
1 vegetable stock cube
400g/14oz can or jar of pimientos
45–60ml/3–4 tbsp tomato purée
115g/4oz pasta shapes
4 pieces French bread
15ml/1 tbsp pesto sauce
115g/4oz/1 cup baby sweetcorn, halved
50g/2oz each broccoli and
    cauliflower florets
few drops of Tabasco sauce, to taste
salt and ground black pepper

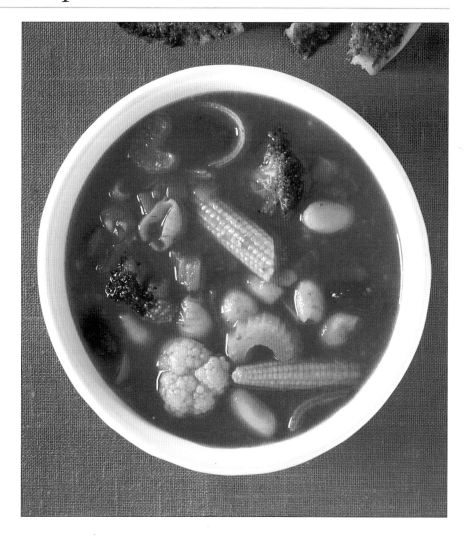

1 Drain the beans and place in a large saucepan with 1.2 litres/ 2 pints/5 cups water. Bring to the boil and simmer for about 1 hour, or until nearly tender.

2 When the beans are almost ready, heat the oil in a large pan and fry the vegetables for 2 minutes. Add the stock cube and the beans with 600ml/1 pint/ 2 cups of their liquid. Cover and simmer for 10 minutes.

3 Meanwhile, purée the pimientos with a little of their liquid and add to the pan. Stir in the tomato purée and pasta and cook for 15 minutes. Preheat the oven to 200°C/400°F/Gas 6.

4 Meanwhile, make the pesto croûtons; spread the French bread with the pesto sauce and bake for 10 minutes, or until crispy

5 When the pasta is just cooked, add the sweetcorn, broccoli and cauliflower florets, Tabasco sauce and seasoning to taste. Heat through for 2–3 minutes and serve at once with the croûtons.

Thai Chicken Soup

*This classic Oriental soup now
enjoys worldwide popularity.*

INGREDIENTS

Serves 4

15ml/1 tbsp vegetable oil

1 garlic clove, finely chopped

2 boneless chicken breasts, about
175g/6oz each, skinned and chopped

2.5ml/½ tsp ground turmeric

1.5ml/¼ tsp hot chilli powder

75g/3oz creamed coconut

900ml/1½ pints/3¾ cups hot
chicken stock

30ml/2 tbsp lemon or lime juice

30ml/2 tbsp crunchy peanut butter

50g/2oz thread egg noodles, broken into
small pieces

15ml/1 tbsp spring onions, finely chopped

15ml/1 tbsp chopped fresh coriander

salt and ground black pepper

30ml/2 tbsp desiccated coconut and
½ fresh red chilli, seeded and finely
chopped, to garnish

1 Heat the oil in a large pan and
fry the garlic for 1 minute until
lightly golden. Add the chicken
and spices and stir-fry for a further
3–4 minutes.

2 Crumble the creamed coconut
into the hot chicken stock and
stir until dissolved. Pour on to the
chicken then add the lemon or
lime juice, peanut butter and egg
noodles.

3 Cover and simmer for about
15 minutes. Add the spring
onions and fresh coriander, then
season well and cook for a further
5 minutes.

4 Meanwhile, place the desiccated coconut and chilli in a
small frying pan and heat for 2–3
minutes, stirring frequently, until
the coconut is lightly browned.

5 Serve the soup in warmed
bowls sprinkled with the fried
coconut and chilli.

Classic Minestrone

This famous Italian soup has been much imitated around the world – with varying results. The home-made version is a delicious revelation and mouthwateringly healthy with pasta, beans and lots of fresh vegetables.

INGREDIENTS

Serves 4

1 large leek, thinly sliced

2 carrots, chopped

1 courgette, thinly sliced

115g/4oz whole green beans, halved

2 celery sticks, thinly sliced

45ml/3 tbsp olive oil

1.5 litres/2½ pints/6¼ cups stock
   or water

400g/14oz can chopped tomatoes

15ml/1 tbsp chopped fresh basil

5ml/1 tsp chopped fresh thyme or
   2.5ml/½ tsp dried

salt and ground black pepper

400g/14oz can cannellini or kidney beans

50g/2oz small pasta shapes or macaroni

finely grated Parmesan cheese, to
   garnish (optional)

fresh parsley, chopped, to garnish

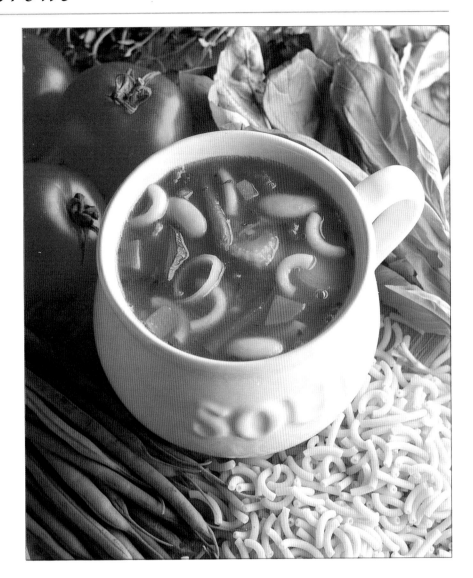

1 Put all the fresh vegetables into a large saucepan with the olive oil. Heat until sizzling then cover, lower the heat and sweat the vegetables for 15 minutes, shaking the pan occasionally.

2 Add the stock or water, tomatoes, herbs and seasoning. Bring to the boil, replace the lid and simmer gently for about 30 minutes.

3 Add the canned beans and their liquor together with the pasta, and simmer for a further 10 minutes. Check the seasoning and serve hot, sprinkled with the Parmesan cheese, if using, and chopped fresh parsley.

COOK'S TIP

Minestrone is also delicious served cold on a hot summer's day. In fact the flavour improves if made a day or two ahead and stored in the fridge. It can also be frozen and reheated.

Fresh Pea and Ham Soup

Frozen peas provide flavour, freshness and colour in this delicious winter soup, which is filling enough to make a light main course or can be served as a starter.

INGREDIENTS

Serves 4

115g/4oz small pasta shapes

30ml/2 tbsp vegetable oil

1 small bunch spring onions, chopped

350g/12oz/3 cups frozen peas

1.2 litres/2 pints/5 cups chicken stock

225g/8oz raw unsmoked ham or gammon

60ml/4 tbsp double cream

salt and ground black pepper

warm crusty bread, to serve

1 Cook the small pasta shapes in plenty of boiling salted water according to the packet instructions. Drain through a colander, place in the pan again, cover with cold water and set aside until required.

2 Heat the vegetable oil in a large heavy saucepan and cook the spring onions gently until soft but not browned. Add the frozen peas and chicken stock, then simmer gently over a low heat for about 10 minutes.

3 Process the soup in a blender or food processor then return to the saucepan. Cut the ham or gammon into short fingers and add, with the pasta, to the saucepan. Simmer for 2–3 minutes and season to taste. Stir in the double cream and serve immediately with the warm crusty bread.

Consommé with Agnolotti

A delicious and satisfying consommé with wonderful flavours.

INGREDIENTS

Serves 4–6

75g/3oz cooked peeled prawns

75g/3oz canned crab meat, drained

5ml/1 tsp fresh root ginger, peeled and finely grated

15ml/1 tbsp fresh white breadcrumbs

5ml/1 tsp light soy sauce

1 spring onion, finely chopped

1 garlic clove, crushed

1 quantity of basic pasta dough

flour, for dusting

egg white, beaten

400g/14oz can chicken or fish consommé

30ml/2 tbsp sherry or vermouth

salt and ground black pepper

50g/2oz cooked, peeled prawns and fresh coriander leaves, to garnish

1 To make the filling, put the prawns, crab meat, ginger, breadcrumbs, soy sauce, onion, garlic and seasoning into a food processor or blender and process until smooth.

2 Roll the pasta into thin sheets and dust lightly with flour. Stamp out 32 rounds 5cm/2in in diameter, with a fluted pastry cutter.

3 Place a small teaspoon of the filling in the centre of half the pasta rounds. Brush the edges of each round with egg white and sandwich together with a second round on top. Pinch the edges together firmly to stop the filling seeping out.

4 Cook the pasta in a large pan of boiling salted water for 5 minutes (cook in batches to stop them sticking together). Remove and drop into a bowl of cold water for 5 seconds before placing on a tray. (You can make these pasta shapes a day in advance. Cover with clear film and store in the fridge until required.)

5 Heat the chicken or fish consommé in a pan with the sherry or vermouth. When piping hot, add the pasta shapes and simmer for 1–2 minutes.

6 Serve in a shallow soup bowl covered with hot consommé. Garnish with extra peeled prawns and fresh coriander leaves.

Red Onion and Beetroot Soup

This beautiful, vivid ruby-red soup will look stunning at any dinner-party table.

INGREDIENTS

Serves 4–6

15ml/1 tbsp olive oil

350g/12oz red onions, sliced

2 garlic cloves, crushed

275g/10oz cooked beetroot, cut into sticks

1.2 litres/2 pints/5 cups vegetable stock
   or water

50g/2oz cooked soup pasta

30ml/2 tbsp raspberry vinegar

salt and ground black pepper

low-fat yogurt or fromage blanc,
   to garnish

snipped chives, to garnish

3 Add the beetroot, stock or water, cooked soup pasta and vinegar, and heat through. Season to taste with salt and pepper.

4 Ladle into warmed soup bowls. Top each one with a spoonful of low-fat yogurt or fromage blanc and sprinkle with chives.

1 Heat the olive oil in a flame-proof casserole and add the onions and garlic.

2 Cook gently for 20 minutes or until the onions and garlic are soft and tender.

Chinese-style Vegetable and Noodle Soup

This soup is wonderfully quick and easy to prepare.

INGREDIENTS

Serves 4

1.2 litres/2 pints/5 cups vegetable or
   chicken stock
1 garlic clove, lightly crushed
2.5cm/1in piece fresh root ginger, peeled
   and cut into fine matchsticks
30ml/2 tbsp soy sauce
15ml/1 tbsp cider vinegar
75g/3oz fresh shiitake or button
   mushrooms, stalks removed and
   thinly sliced
2 large spring onions, thinly sliced on
   the diagonal
40g/1½oz vermicelli or other fine noodles
175g/6oz Chinese leaves, shredded
a few fresh coriander leaves

1 Pour the stock into a saucepan. Add the garlic, root ginger, soy sauce and vinegar. Bring to the boil, then cover the pan and reduce the heat to very low. Leave to simmer gently for 10 minutes. Remove the garlic clove from the pan and discard.

2 Add the sliced mushrooms and spring onions and bring the soup back to the boil. Simmer for 5 minutes, uncovered, stirring occasionally. Add the noodles and shredded Chinese leaves. Simmer for 3–4 minutes, or until the noodles and vegetables are just tender. Stir in the coriander leaves. Simmer for a final 1 minute. Serve the soup hot.

Chicken Vermicelli Soup with Egg Shreds

*This soup is very quick and easy –
you can add all sorts of extra
ingredients to vary the taste, using
up leftovers such as spring
onions, mushrooms, a few prawns
or chopped salami.*

INGREDIENTS

Serves 4–6

3 eggs

30ml/2 tbsp chopped fresh coriander
    or parsley

1.5 litres/2½ pints/6¼ cups good chicken
    stock or canned consommé

115g/4oz dried vermicelli or angel
    hair pasta

115g/4oz cooked chicken breast, sliced

salt and ground black pepper

1 First make the egg shreds.
Whisk the eggs together in a
small bowl and stir in the
coriander or parsley.

2 Heat a small non-stick frying
pan and pour in 30–45ml/
2–3 tbsp egg, swirling to cover the
base evenly. Cook until set. Repeat
until all the mixture is used up.

3 Roll each pancake up and slice
thinly into shreds. Set aside.

4 Bring the stock or consommé
to the boil and add the pasta,
breaking it up into short lengths.
Cook for 3–5 minutes until the

pasta is almost tender, then add the
chicken, and salt and pepper to
taste. Heat through for about
2–3 minutes, then stir in the egg
shreds. Serve immediately.

THAI CHICKEN SOUP

To make a Thai variation, use
Chinese rice noodles instead of
pasta. Stir 1.5ml/½ tsp dried lemon
grass, 2 small whole fresh chillies
and 60ml/4 tbsp coconut milk into
the stock. Add 4 sliced spring
onions and plenty of chopped
fresh coriander.

Parmesan and Cauliflower Soup

A silky smooth, mildly cheesy soup which isn't overpowered by the cauliflower. It makes an elegant dinner-party soup served with crisp Melba toast.

INGREDIENTS

Serves 6

1 large cauliflower

1.2 litres/2 pints/5 cups chicken or
    vegetable stock

175g/6oz farfalle

150ml/¼ pint/⅔ cup single cream or milk

freshly grated nutmeg

pinch of cayenne pepper

60ml/4 tbsp freshly grated
    Parmesan cheese

salt and ground black pepper

For the Melba toast

3–4 slices day-old white bread

freshly grated Parmesan cheese,
    for sprinkling

1.5ml/¼ tsp paprika

3 Add the pasta to the stock and simmer for 10 minutes until tender. Drain, reserve the pasta, and pour the liquid over the cauliflower. Add the cream or milk, nutmeg and cayenne to the cauliflower. Blend until smooth, then press through a sieve. Stir in the cooked pasta. Reheat the soup and stir in the Parmesan. Taste and adjust the seasoning if necessary.

4 Meanwhile make the Melba toast. Preheat the oven to 180°C/350°F/Gas 4. Toast the bread lightly on both sides. Quickly cut off the crusts and split each slice in half horizontally. Scrape off any doughy bits and sprinkle with Parmesan and paprika. Place on a baking sheet and bake in the oven for about 10–15 minutes or until uniformly golden. Serve with the soup.

1 Cut the leaves and central stalk away from the cauliflower and discard. Divide the cauliflower into similar-size florets.

2 Bring the stock to the boil and add the cauliflower. Simmer for about 10 minutes or until very soft. Remove the cauliflower with a slotted spoon and place in a blender or food processor.

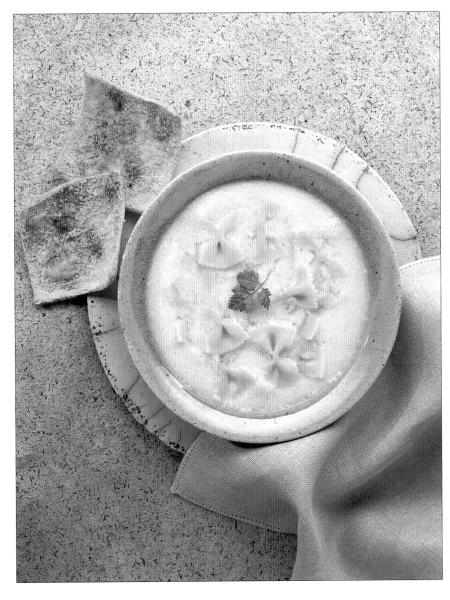

Italian Bean and Pasta Soup

A thick and hearty soup which, followed by bread and cheese, makes a substantial lunch.

Serves 6

175g/6oz/1½ cups dried haricot beans, soaked overnight in cold water

1.75 litres/3 pints/7½ cups chicken stock or water

115g/4oz medium pasta shells

60ml/4 tbsp olive oil, plus extra to serve

2 garlic cloves, crushed

60ml/4 tbsp chopped fresh parsley

salt and ground black pepper

1 Drain the beans and place in a large saucepan with the stock or water. Simmer, half-covered, for 2–2½ hours or until tender.

2 In a blender or food processor, process half the beans with a little of their cooking liquid, then stir into the unprocessed beans in the pan.

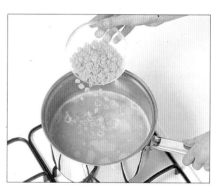

3 Add the pasta and simmer gently for 15 minutes until tender. (Add extra water or stock if the soup seems too thick.)

4 Heat the oil in a small pan and fry the garlic until golden. Stir into the soup with the parsley and season well with salt and pepper. Ladle into individual bowls and drizzle each with a little extra olive oil, to serve.

Courgette Soup with Small Pasta Shells

A pretty, fresh-tasting soup which could be made using cucumber instead of courgettes.

Serves 4–6

60ml/4 tbsp olive or sunflower oil

2 onions, finely chopped

1.5 litres/2½ pints/6¼ cups chicken stock

900g/2lb courgettes

115g/4oz small soup pasta

freshly squeezed lemon juice

30ml/2 tbsp chopped fresh chervil

salt and ground black pepper

soured cream, to serve

1 Heat the oil in a large saucepan and add the onions. Cover and cook gently for about 20 minutes until very soft but not coloured, stirring occasionally.

2 Add the chicken stock to the saucepan and bring the mixture to the boil.

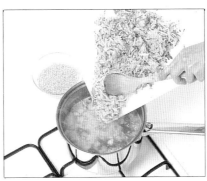

3 Meanwhile grate the courgettes and stir into the boiling stock with the pasta. Reduce the heat and simmer for 15 minutes until the pasta is tender. Season to taste with lemon juice, salt and pepper.

4 Stir in the chopped fresh chervil and add a swirl of soured cream before serving.

Minestrone

A substantial and popular winter soup originally from Milan, but found in various versions around the Mediterranean coasts of Italy and France. Cut the vegetables as roughly or as small as you like. Add freshly grated Parmesan cheese just before serving.

INGREDIENTS

Serves 6–8

225g/8oz/2 cups dried haricot beans

30ml/2 tbsp olive oil

50g/2oz smoked streaky bacon, diced

2 large onions, sliced

2 garlic cloves, crushed

2 carrots, diced

3 celery sticks, sliced

400g/14oz canned chopped tomatoes

2.25 litres/4 pints/10 cups beef stock

350g/12oz potatoes, diced

175g/6oz small pasta shapes, such as
    macaroni, stars, shells, etc

225g/8oz green cabbage, thinly sliced

175g/6oz fine green beans, sliced

115g/4oz/1 cup frozen peas

45ml/3 tbsp chopped fresh parsley

salt and ground black pepper

freshly grated Parmesan cheese, to serve

1 Cover the beans with cold water in a bowl and leave to soak overnight.

2 Heat the oil in a large saucepan and add the bacon, onions and garlic. Cover and cook gently for 5 minutes, stirring occasionally.

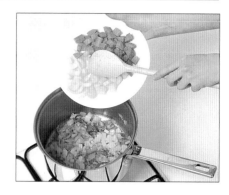

3 Add the carrots and celery and cook for 2–3 minutes until the vegetables are softening.

4 Drain the beans and add to the pan with the tomatoes and the beef stock. Cover and simmer for 2–2½ hours, until the beans are tender.

5 Add the potatoes 30 minutes before the soup is ready.

6 Add the pasta, cabbage, beans, peas and parsley 15 minutes before the soup is ready. Season to taste and serve with a bowl of freshly grated Parmesan cheese.

Provençal Fish Soup with Pasta

This colourful soup has all the flavours of the Mediterranean. Serve it as a main course for a deliciously filling lunch.

INGREDIENTS

Serves 4

30ml/2 tbsp olive oil

1 onion, sliced

1 garlic clove, crushed

1 leek, sliced

225g/8oz canned chopped tomatoes

pinch of Mediterranean herbs

1.5ml/¼ tsp saffron strands (optional)

115g/4oz small pasta

about 8 live mussels in the shell

450g/1lb filleted and skinned white fish, such as cod, plaice or monkfish

salt and ground black pepper

For the rouille

2 garlic cloves, crushed

1 canned pimiento, drained and chopped

15ml/1 tbsp fresh white breadcrumbs

60ml/4 tbsp mayonnaise

toasted French bread, to serve

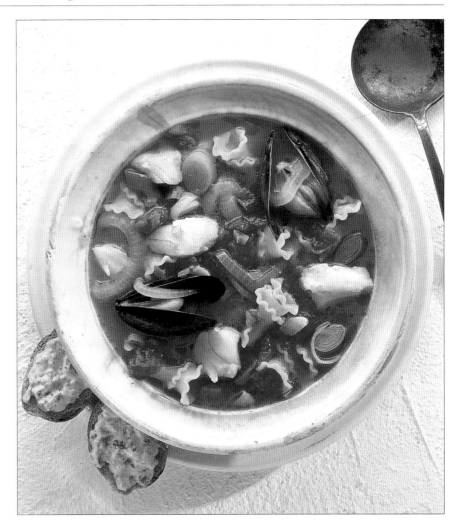

1 Heat the oil in a large saucepan and add the onion, garlic and leek. Cover and cook gently for 5 minutes, stirring occasionally until the vegetables are soft.

2 Pour in 1 litre/1¾pints/4 cups water, the tomatoes, herbs, saffron and pasta. Season with salt and ground black pepper and cook for 15–20 minutes.

3 Scrub the mussels and pull off the "beards". Discard any that will not close when sharply tapped.

4 Cut the fish into bite-size chunks and add to the soup, placing the mussels on top. Then simmer with the lid on for 5-10 minutes until the mussels open and the fish is just cooked. Discard any unopened mussels.

5 To make the rouille, pound the garlic, canned pimiento and breadcrumbs together in a pestle and mortar (or in a blender or food processor). Stir in the mayonnaise and season well.

6 Spread the toasted French bread with the rouille and serve with the soup.

PASTA WITH
FISH &
SHELLFISH

Salmon Pasta with Parsley Sauce

This dish is so quick and easy to make – and delicious.

INGREDIENTS

Serves 4

450g/1lb salmon fillet, skinned

225g/8oz pasta, such as penne or twists

175g/6oz cherry tomatoes, halved

150ml/¼ pint/⅔ cup low -fat
   crème fraîche

45ml/3 tbsp finely chopped parsley

finely grated rind of ½ orange

salt and ground black pepper

1 Cut the salmon into bite-size pieces, arrange on a heatproof plate and cover with foil.

2 Bring a large pan of salted water to the boil, add the pasta and return to the boil. Place the plate of salmon on top and simmer for 10–12 minutes, until the pasta and salmon are cooked.

3 Drain the pasta and toss with the tomatoes and salmon. Mix together the crème fraîche, parsley, orange rind and pepper to taste, then toss into the salmon and pasta and serve hot or cold.

Tagliatelle with Saffron Mussels

Mussels in a saffron and cream sauce are served with tagliatelle in this recipe, but you can use any other pasta if you prefer.

Serves 4

1.75kg/4–4½lb live mussels in the shell

150ml/¼ pint/⅔ cup dry white wine

2 shallots, chopped

350g/12oz dried tagliatelle

25g/1oz/2 tbsp butter

2 garlic cloves, crushed

250ml/8fl oz/1 cup double cream

generous pinch of saffron strands

1 egg yolk

salt and ground black pepper

30ml/2 tbsp chopped fresh parsley,
   to garnish

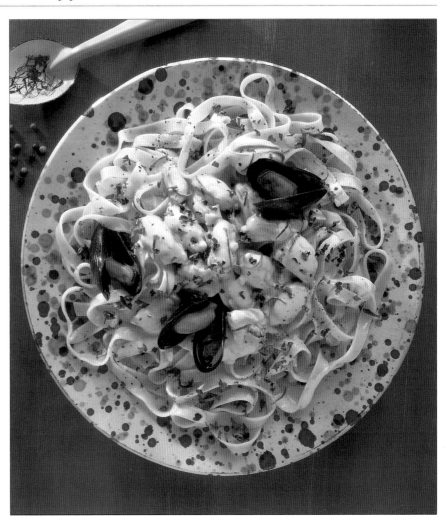

1 Scrub the mussels well under cold running water. Remove the "beards" and discard any mussels that are open.

2 Place the mussels in a large pan with the wine and shallots. Cover and cook over a high heat, shaking the pan occasionally, for 5-8 minutes until the mussels have opened. Drain the mussels, reserving the liquid. Discard any that remain closed. Shell all but a few of the mussels and keep warm.

3 Bring the reserved cooking liquid to the boil, then reduce by half. Strain into a jug to remove any grit.

4 Cook the tagliatelle in plenty of boiling salted water for about 10 minutes, until *al dente*.

5 Meanwhile, melt the butter and fry the garlic for 1 minute. Pour in the mussel liquid, cream and saffron strands. Heat gently until the sauce thickens slightly. Off the heat, stir in the egg yolk, shelled mussels, and season.

6 Drain the tagliatelle and transfer to warmed serving bowls. Spoon the sauce over and sprinkle with chopped parsley. Garnish with the mussels in shells and serve at once.

Spaghetti with Tomato and Clam Sauce

Small sweet clams make this a delicately succulent sauce. Cockles would make a good substitute, or even mussels, but don't be tempted to use seafood pickled in vinegar.

INGREDIENTS

Serves 4

900g/2lb live small clams in the shell, or 2 x 400g/14oz cans clams in brine, drained
90ml/6 tbsp olive oil
2 garlic cloves, crushed
500g/1¼lb canned chopped tomatoes
45ml/3 tbsp chopped fresh parsley
450g/1lb spaghetti
salt and ground black pepper

1 If using live clams, place them in a bowl of cold water and rinse several times to remove any grit or sand, then drain well.

2 Heat the oil in a saucepan and add the clams. Stir over a high heat until the clams open. Discard any that do not open. Transfer the clams to a bowl with a slotted spoon and set aside.

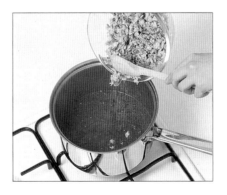

3 Reduce the clam juice left in the pan to almost nothing by boiling fast. Add the garlic and fry until golden. Pour in the tomatoes, bring to the boil and cook for 3–4 minutes until reduced. Stir in the clam mixture or canned clams and half the parsley and heat through. Season to taste.

4 Cook the pasta in plenty of boiling salted water according to the instructions on the packet. Drain well and turn into a warm serving dish. Pour over the sauce and sprinkle with the remaining chopped parsley.

Spaghetti with Clams

Try chopped fresh dill for a delicious alternative in this dish.

INGREDIENTS

Serves 4

24 live clams in the shell, scrubbed
250ml/8fl oz/1 cup water
120ml/4fl oz/½ cup dry white wine
450g/1lb spaghetti, preferably Italian
75ml/5 tbsp olive oil
2 garlic cloves, minced
45ml/3 tbsp chopped fresh parsley
salt and ground black pepper

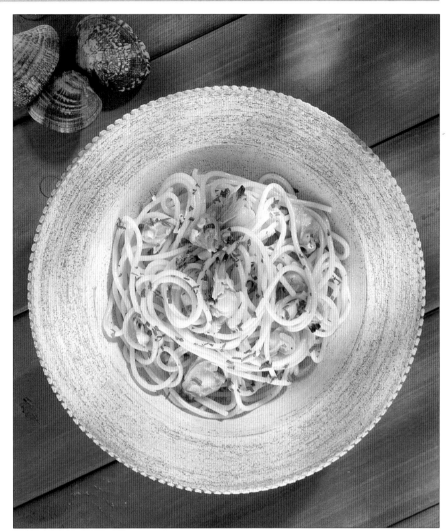

1 Rinse the clams well in cold water and drain. Place in a large saucepan with the water and wine and bring to the boil. Cover and steam until the shells open, about 6–8 minutes.

2 Discard any clams that have not opened. Remove the clams from their shells. If large, chop them roughly.

3 Strain the cooking liquid through a strainer lined with muslin. Place in a small saucepan and boil rapidly until reduced by about half. Set aside.

4 Cook the spaghetti in plenty of boiling salted water according to the instructions on the packet until *al dente*.

5 Meanwhile, heat the olive oil in a large frying pan. Add the garlic and cook for 2–3 minutes, but do not let it brown. Add the reduced clam liquid and the parsley. Cook over a low heat until the spaghetti is ready.

6 Drain the spaghetti. Add to the frying pan, increase the heat to medium, and add the clams. Cook for 3–4 minutes, stirring, to coat the spaghetti with the sauce and to heat the clams.

7 Season with salt and pepper and serve at once.

Pasta with Tuna, Capers and Anchovies

This piquant sauce could be made without the addition of tomatoes – just heat the oil, add the other ingredients and heat through gently before tossing with the pasta.

INGREDIENTS

Serves 4

400g/14oz can tuna fish in oil

30ml/2 tbsp olive oil

2 garlic cloves, crushed

800g/1¾lb canned chopped tomatoes

6 canned anchovy fillets, drained

30ml/2 tbsp capers in vinegar, drained

30ml/2 tbsp chopped fresh basil

450g/1lb rigatoni, penne or garganelle

salt and ground black pepper

fresh basil sprigs, to garnish

1 Drain the oil from the can of tuna fish into a large saucepan, add the olive oil and heat gently until the oil mixture stops spitting.

2 Add the garlic and fry until golden. Stir in the tomatoes and simmer for about 25 minutes until thickened.

3 Flake the tuna and cut the anchovies in half. Stir into the sauce with the capers and chopped basil. Season well.

4 Cook the pasta in plenty of boiling salted water according to the instructions on the packet. Drain well and toss with the sauce. Garnish with fresh basil sprigs.

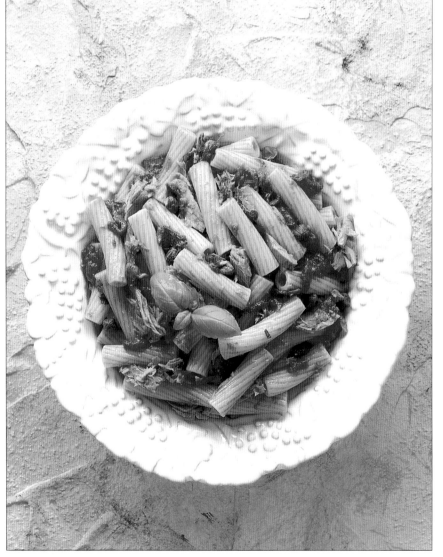

Noodles with Prawns in Lemon Sauce

As in many Chinese dishes the fish is here purely for colour and flavour.

INGREDIENTS

Serves 4

2 packets Chinese egg noodles

15ml/1 tbsp sunflower oil

2 celery sticks, cut into matchsticks

2 garlic cloves, crushed

4 spring onions, sliced

2 carrots, cut into matchsticks

7.5cm/3in piece cucumber, cut
   into matchsticks

115g/4oz prawns in the shells

1 lemon

30ml/2 tbsp lemon juice or sauce

5ml/1 tsp cornflour

60–75ml/4–5 tbsp fish stock

115g/4oz/1 cup shelled prawns

salt and ground black pepper

a few sprigs dill, to garnish

1 Put the noodles in boiling water and leave to soak as directed on the packet. Meanwhile, heat the oil in a pan and stir-fry the celery, garlic, spring onions and carrots for 2–3 minutes.

COOK'S TIP

These noodles can be deep-fried. Cook as above; drain on kitchen paper. Deep-fry in batches until golden and crisp.

2 Add the cucumber and whole prawns and cook for about 2–3 minutes. Meanwhile, peel the rind from the lemon and cut into long thin shreds. Place in boiling water for 1 minute.

3 Blend the lemon juice, or lemon sauce, with the cornflour and stock and add to the pan. Bring gently to the boil, stirring, and cook for 1 minute.

4 Stir in the shelled prawns, the drained lemon rind and seasoning to taste. Drain the noodles and serve with the prawns, garnished with dill.

Seafood Pasta Shells with Spinach Sauce

You'll need very large pasta shells, measuring about 4cm/1½in long for this dish; don't try stuffing smaller shells – they will be much too fiddly!

INGREDIENTS

Serves 4

15g/½oz/1 tbsp margarine

8 spring onions, finely sliced

6 tomatoes

32 large dried pasta shells

225g/8oz/1 cup low-fat soft cheese

90ml/6 tbsp skimmed milk

pinch of freshly grated nutmeg

225g/8oz/2 cups prawns

175g/6oz can white crab meat, drained and flaked

115g/4oz frozen chopped spinach, thawed and drained

salt and ground black pepper

2 Slash the bottoms of the tomatoes, plunge into a saucepan of boiling water for 45 seconds, then into a saucepan of cold water. Slip off the skins. Halve the tomatoes, remove the seeds and cores and roughly chop the flesh.

5 Add the spring onions, tomatoes, prawns, and crab meat to the bowl. Mix well. Spoon the filling into the shells and place in a single layer in a shallow ovenproof dish. Cover with foil and cook in the preheated oven for 10 minutes.

1 Preheat the oven to 150°C/ 300°F/Gas 2. Melt the margarine in a small saucepan and gently cook the spring onions for 3–4 minutes, or until softened.

3 Cook the pasta shells in plenty of boiling salted water for about 10 minutes, or until *al dente*. Drain well.

6 Stir the spinach into the remaining sauce. Bring to the boil and simmer gently for 1 minute, stirring all the time. Drizzle over the pasta shells and serve hot.

4 Heat the soft cheese and milk in a saucepan, stirring until blended. Season with salt, pepper and nutmeg. Measure 30ml/2 tbsp of the sauce into a bowl.

Pasta Bows with Smoked Salmon and Dill

In Italy, pasta cooked with smoked salmon is very fashionable. This is a quick and luxurious sauce.

INGREDIENTS

Serves 4

6 spring onions

50g/2oz/4 tbsp butter

90ml/6 tbsp dry white wine or vermouth

450ml/¾ pint/1¾ cups double cream

freshly grated nutmeg

225g/8oz smoked salmon

30ml/2 tbsp chopped fresh dill or
   15ml/1 tbsp dried

freshly squeezed lemon juice

450g/1lb farfalle

salt and ground black pepper

1 Slice the spring onions finely. Melt the butter in a saucepan and gently fry the spring onions for 1 minute until softened.

2 Add the wine or vermouth and boil hard to reduce to about 30ml/2 tbsp. Stir in the cream and add salt, pepper and nutmeg to taste. Bring to the boil and simmer for 2–3 minutes until the sauce is slightly thickened.

3 Cut the smoked salmon into 2.5cm/1in squares and stir into the sauce with the dill. Taste and add a little lemon juice. Keep the sauce warm.

4 Cook the pasta in plenty of boiling salted water according to the instructions on the packet. Drain well. Toss the pasta with the sauce and serve immediately.

Spaghetti with Mixed Shellfish Sauce

A special occasion sauce for an evening of entertaining is just what this is, so serve it in bountiful portions to your guests.

INGREDIENTS

Serves 4

50g/2oz/4 tbsp butter

2 shallots, chopped

2 garlic cloves, chopped

350g/12oz spaghetti

2 tbsp finely chopped fresh basil

300ml/½ pint/1¼ cups dry white wine

450g/1lb mussels, scrubbed

115g/4oz squid, washed

5ml/1 tsp chilli powder

350g/12oz raw peeled prawns

300ml/½ pint/1¼ cups soured cream

salt and ground black pepper

50g/2oz/⅓ cup Parmesan cheese,
   freshly grated

chopped fresh flat leaf parsley, to garnish

to the pan, cover and simmer for about 5 minutes until all the shells have opened. Discard any mussels that do not open. Using a slotted spoon, transfer the mussels to a plate, remove them from their shells and return to the pan. Reserve a few mussels in the shells for garnishing.

5 Meanwhile, slice the squid into thin circles. Melt the remaining butter in a frying pan and fry the remaining shallot and garlic for about 5 minutes until softened.

6 Add the remaining basil, the squid, chilli powder and prawns to the pan and stir-fry for 5 minutes until the prawns have turned pink and tender.

7 Turn the mussel mixture into the prawn mixture and bring to the boil. Stir in the soured cream and season to taste. Bring almost to the boil and simmer for 1 minute.

8 Drain the pasta thoroughly and stir it into the sauce with the Parmesan cheese until well coated. Serve immediately, garnished with chopped flat leaf parsley and the reserved mussels in their shells.

1 Melt half the butter in a frying pan and fry 1 shallot and 1 garlic clove for about 5 minutes until softened

2 Cook the pasta in plenty of boiling salted water according to the instructions on the packet.

3 Stir in half the basil and the wine and bring to the boil.

4 Discard any mussels that are open and do not shut when tapped with the back of a knife. Quickly add the remaining mussels

Pasta with Spinach and Anchovy Sauce

Deliciously earthy, this would make a good starter or light supper dish. Add some sultanas to the sauce to ring the changes.

INGREDIENTS

Serves 4

900g/2lb fresh spinach or 500g/1¼lb
    frozen leaf spinach, thawed
450g/1lb angel hair pasta
salt, to taste
60ml/4 tbsp olive oil
45ml/3 tbsp pine nuts
2 garlic cloves
6 canned anchovy fillets, drained and
    chopped, or whole salted anchovies,
    rinsed, boned and chopped
butter, for tossing the pasta

1 If using fresh spinach, wash it well and remove any tough stalks. Drain thoroughly. Place in a large saucepan with only the water that clings to the leaves. Cover with a lid and cook over a high heat, shaking the pan occasionally, until the spinach is just wilted and still bright green. Drain.

2 Cook the pasta in plenty of boiling salted water according to the instructions on the packet.

3 Heat the oil in a saucepan and fry the pine nuts until golden. Remove with a slotted spoon. Add the garlic to the oil in the pan and fry until golden. Add the chopped anchovies to the pan.

4 Stir in the spinach and cook for 2–3 minutes or until heated through. Stir in the pine nuts. Drain the pasta, toss in a little butter and turn into a warmed serving dish. Top with the hot sauce and fork through roughly before serving.

Tagliatelle with Haddock and Avocado

You will need to start this recipe the day before because the haddock should be left to marinate overnight.

Serves 4

350g/12oz fresh haddock fillets, skinned

2.5ml/½ tsp each ground cumin, ground coriander and turmeric

150ml/¼ pint/⅔ cup fromage frais

150ml/¼ pint/⅔ cup double cream

15ml/1 tbsp lemon juice

25g/1oz/2 tbsp butter

1 onion, chopped

15ml/1 tbsp plain flour

150ml/¼ pint/⅔ cup fish stock

350g/12oz tagliatelle

1 avocado, peeled, stoned and sliced

2 tomatoes, seeded and chopped

salt and ground black pepper

fresh rosemary sprigs, to garnish

1 Carefully cut the haddock into bite-size pieces.

2 Mix together all the spices, seasoning, fromage frais, cream and lemon juice.

3 Stir in the haddock to coat. Cover the dish and leave to marinate overnight.

4 Heat the butter in a frying pan and fry the onion for about 10 minutes until softened. Stir in the flour, then blend in the stock until smooth.

5 Carefully stir in the haddock mixture until well blended. Bring to the boil, stirring, cover and simmer for about 30 seconds. Remove from the heat.

6 Meanwhile, cook the pasta in plenty of boiling salted water according to the instructions on the packet.

7 Stir the avocado and tomatoes into the haddock mixture.

8 Drain the pasta thoroughly and divide among four serving plates. Spoon over the sauce and serve immediately, garnished with fresh rosemary.

Smoked Trout Cannelloni

Smoked trout can be bought already filleted or whole. If you buy fillets, you'll need 225g/8oz.

INGREDIENTS

Serves 4–6

1 large onion, finely chopped
1 garlic clove, crushed
60ml/4 tbsp vegetable stock
2 x 400g/14oz cans chopped tomatoes
2.5ml/½ tsp dried mixed herbs
1 smoked trout, about 400g/14oz
75g/3oz/¾ cup frozen peas, thawed
75g/3oz/1½ cups fresh breadcrumbs
16 cannelloni tubes
salt and ground black pepper
mixed salad, to serve (optional)
25ml/1½ tbsp freshly grated
  Parmesan cheese

For the cheese sauce
25g/1oz/2 tbsp margarine
25g/1oz/¼ cup plain flour
350ml/12fl oz/1½ cups skimmed milk
freshly grated nutmeg

1 Simmer the onion, garlic and stock in a large covered saucepan for 3 minutes. Uncover and continue to cook, stirring occasionally, until the stock has reduced entirely.

2 Stir in the tomatoes and dried herbs. Simmer, uncovered, for a further 10 minutes, or until the mixture is very thick.

3 Meanwhile, skin the smoked trout with a sharp knife. Carefully flake the flesh and discard the bones. Mix the fish together with the tomato mixture, peas, breadcrumbs, salt and ground black pepper.

4 Preheat the oven to 190°C/ 375°F/Gas 5. Spoon the filling into the cannelloni tubes and arrange in an ovenproof dish.

5 For the sauce, put the margarine, flour and milk into a saucepan and cook over a medium heat, whisking constantly until the sauce thickens. Simmer for 2–3 minutes, stirring all the time. Season to taste with salt, pepper and nutmeg.

6 Pour the sauce over the cannelloni and sprinkle with the grated Parmesan cheese. Bake in the oven for 35–40 minutes, or until the top is golden and bubbling. Serve with a mixed salad, if desired.

Pasta with Scallops and Tomato Sauce

Fresh basil gives this sauce a distinctive flavour.

INGREDIENTS

Serves 4

450g/1lb pasta, such as fettucine
   or linguine
30ml/2 tbsp olive oil
2 garlic cloves, crushed
450g/1lb sea scallops, halved horizontally
salt and ground black pepper
30ml/2 tbsp chopped fresh basil

For the sauce

30ml/2 tbsp olive oil
½ onion, minced
1 garlic clove, crushed
2.5ml/½ tsp salt
2 x 400g/14oz cans plum tomatoes

1 For the sauce, heat the oil in a non-stick frying pan. Add the onion, garlic and a little salt, and cook over a medium heat for about 5 minutes until just softened, stirring occasionally.

2 Add the tomatoes, with their juice, and crush with a fork. Bring to the boil, then reduce the heat and simmer gently for 15 minutes. Remove from the heat and set aside.

3 Cook the pasta in plenty of boiling salted water, according to the instructions on the packet, until *al dente*.

4 Meanwhile, combine the oil and garlic in another non-stick frying pan and cook until just sizzling, about 30 seconds. Add the scallops and 2.5ml/½ tsp salt and cook over a high heat, tossing until the scallops are cooked through, about 3 minutes.

5 Add the scallops to the tomato sauce. Season with salt and pepper, stir and keep warm.

6 Drain the pasta, rinse under hot water and drain again. Place in a large serving dish. Add the sauce and the basil and toss thoroughly. Serve immediately.

Baked Seafood Spaghetti

In this dish, each portion is baked and served in an individual packet which is then opened at the table. Use baking parchment paper or foil to make the packets.

INGREDIENTS

Serves 4

450g/1lb fresh mussels

120ml/4fl oz/½ cup dry white wine

60ml/4 tbsp olive oil

2 garlic cloves, finely chopped

450g/1lb tomatoes, fresh or canned, peeled and finely chopped

400g/14oz spaghetti or other long pasta

225g/8oz/2 cups peeled and deveined prawns, fresh or frozen

30ml/2 tbsp chopped fresh parsley

salt and ground black pepper

1 Scrub the mussels well under cold running water, cutting off the "beards" with a small sharp knife. Discard any that do not close when tapped sharply. Place the mussels and the wine in a large saucepan and heat until opened.

2 Lift out the mussels and remove to a side dish. Discard any that do not open. Strain the cooking liquid into a bowl through kitchen paper and reserve until needed. Preheat the oven to 150°C/300°F/Gas 2.

3 In a medium saucepan, heat the oil and garlic together for 1–2 minutes. Add the tomatoes and cook over a moderate to high heat until softened. Stir 175ml/6fl oz/¾ cup of the mussel cooking liquid into the saucepan.

4 Cook the pasta in plenty of boiling salted water until just *al dente.* Just before draining the pasta, add the prawns and parsley to the tomato sauce. Cook for 2 minutes. Taste for seasoning, adding salt and pepper if necessary. Remove from the heat.

5 Prepare four pieces of baking parchment paper or foil about 30 × 45cm/12 × 18in. Place each sheet in the centre of a shallow bowl. Turn the drained pasta into a mixing bowl. Add the tomato sauce and mix well. Stir in the mussels.

6 Divide the pasta and seafood among the four pieces of paper or foil, placing a mound in the centre of each, and twisting the ends together to make a closed packet. Arrange on a large baking sheet and place in the centre of the oven. Bake for 8–10 minutes. Place the unopened packets on individual serving plates.

Fusilli with Vegetable and Prawn Sauce

You will need to start this recipe the day before because the prawns should be left to marinate overnight.

INGREDIENTS

Serves 4

450g/1lb/4 cups peeled prawns

60ml/4 tbsp soy sauce

45ml/3 tbsp olive oil

350g/12oz curly spaghetti (fusilli col buco)

1 yellow pepper, cored, seeded and cut into strips

225g/8oz broccoli florets

1 bunch spring onions, shredded

2.5cm/1in piece fresh ginger root, peeled and shredded

15ml/1 tbsp chopped fresh oregano

30ml/2 tbsp dry sherry

15ml/1 tbsp cornflour

300ml/½ pint/1¼ cups fish stock

salt and ground black pepper

1 Place the prawns in a mixing bowl. Stir in half the soy sauce and 30ml/2 tbsp of the olive oil. Cover and marinate overnight.

2 Cook the pasta in plenty of boiling salted water according to the instructions on the packet.

3 Meanwhile, heat the remaining oil in a wok or frying pan and fry the prawns for 1 minute.

4 Add the pepper, broccoli, spring onions, ginger and oregano and stir-fry for about 1–2 minutes.

5 Drain the pasta thoroughly, set aside and keep warm. Meanwhile, blend together the sherry and cornflour until smooth. Stir in the stock and remaining soy sauce until well blended.

6 Pour the sauce into the wok or pan, bring to the boil and stir-fry for 2 minutes until thickened. Pour over the pasta and serve.

Tuna Lasagne

INGREDIENTS

Serves 6

1 quantity fresh pasta dough, cut for
  lasagne, or 375g/12oz no-precook
  dried lasagne
15g/½oz butter
1 small onion, finely chopped
1 garlic clove, finely chopped
115g/4oz mushrooms, thinly sliced
60ml/4 tbsp dry white wine (optional)
600ml/1 pint/2½ cups white sauce
150ml/¼ pint/⅔ cup whipping cream
45ml/3 tbsp chopped parsley
2 x 200g/7oz cans tuna, drained
2 canned pimientos, cut into strips
65g/2½oz/generous ½ cup frozen
  peas, thawed
115g/4oz mozzarella cheese, grated
30ml/2 tbsp freshly grated
  Parmesan cheese
salt and ground black pepper

1 For fresh lasagne, bring a large pan of salted water to the boil. Cook the lasagne, in small batches, until almost tender to the bite. For dried lasagne, soak in a bowl of hot water for 3–5 minutes.

2 Place the lasagne in a colander and rinse with cold water. Lay on a dish towel to drain.

3 Preheat the oven to 180°C/ 350°F//Gas 4. Melt the butter in a saucepan and cook the onion until soft.

4 Add the garlic and mushrooms, and cook until soft, stirring occasionally. Pour in the wine, if using. Boil for 1 minute. Add the white sauce, cream and parsley. Season.

5 Spoon a thin layer of sauce over the base of a 30 × 23cm/ 12 × 9in baking dish. Cover with a layer of lasagne sheets.

6 Flake the tuna. Scatter half the tuna, pimiento strips, peas and mozzarella over the lasagne. Spoon one-third of the remaining sauce over the top, cover with another layer of lasagne sheets.

7 Repeat the layers, ending with pasta and sauce. Sprinkle with the Parmesan. Bake for 30–40 minutes or until lightly browned.

Pasta Tubes with Tuna and Olive Sauce

This colourful sauce combines well with a thicker and shorter pasta.

INGREDIENTS

Serves 4

350g/12oz rigatoni

30ml/2 tbsp olive oil

1 onion, chopped

2 garlic cloves, chopped

400g/14oz can chopped tomatoes

50g/2oz/4 tbsp tomato purée

50g/2oz/½ cup stoned black
    olives, quartered

15ml/1 tbsp chopped fresh oregano

225g/8oz can tuna in oil, drained
    and flaked

2.5ml/½ tsp anchovy purée

15ml/1 tbsp capers, rinsed

115g/4oz/1 cup grated Cheddar cheese

45ml/3 tbsp fresh white breadcrumbs

salt and ground black pepper

flat leaf parsley sprigs, to garnish

1 Cook the pasta in plenty of boiling salted water according to the instructions on the packet.

2 Meanwhile, heat the oil in a frying pan and fry the onion and garlic for about 10 minutes until softened.

3 Add the tomatoes, tomato purée, and salt and pepper, and bring to the boil. Simmer gently for 5 minutes, stirring occasionally.

4 Stir in the olives, oregano, tuna, anchovy purée and capers. Spoon the mixture into a mixing bowl.

5 Drain the pasta, toss well in the sauce and spoon into flame-proof serving dishes.

6 Preheat the grill and sprinkle the cheese and breadcrumbs over the pasta. Grill for about 10 minutes until the pasta is heated through and the cheese has melted. Serve at once, garnished with flat leaf parsley.

Spaghetti with Hot-and-sour Fish

A truly Chinese spicy taste is what makes this sauce so different.

INGREDIENTS

Serves 4

350g/12oz spaghetti

450g/1lb monkfish, skinned

225g/8oz courgettes

1 green chilli, cored and seeded (optional)

15ml/1 tbsp olive oil

1 large onion, chopped

5ml/1 tsp turmeric

115g/4oz/1 cup shelled peas, thawed
   if frozen

10ml/2 tsp lemon juice

75ml/5 tbsp hoisin sauce

150ml/¼ pint/⅔ cup water

salt and ground black pepper

fresh dill sprig, to garnish

1 Cook the pasta in plenty of boiling salted water according to the instructions on the packet.

2 Cut the monkfish into bite-size pieces. Thinly slice the courgettes, then finely chop the chilli, if using.

3 Heat the oil in a large frying pan and fry the onion for 5 minutes until softened. Add the turmeric.

4 Add the chilli, if using, courgettes and peas, and fry over a medium heat for 5 minutes until the vegetables have softened.

5 Stir in the fish, lemon juice, hoisin sauce and water. Bring to the boil, then simmer, uncovered, for about 5 minutes or until the fish is tender. Season.

6 Drain the pasta thoroughly and turn into a serving dish. Toss in the sauce to coat. Serve at once, garnished with fresh dill.

Saffron Pappardelle

A wonderful dish with a delicious shellfish sauce.

INGREDIENTS

Serves 4

large pinch saffron strands

4 sun-dried tomatoes, chopped

5ml/1 tsp fresh thyme

12 large prawns in their shells

225g/8oz baby squid

225g/8oz monkfish fillet

2–3 garlic cloves

2 small onions, quartered

1 small bulb fennel, trimmed and sliced

150ml/¼ pint/⅔ cup white wine

225g/8oz pappardelle

salt and ground black pepper

30ml/2 tbsp chopped fresh parsley,
  to garnish

1 Put the saffron, sun-dried tomatoes and thyme into a bowl with 60ml/4 tbsp hot water. Leave to soak for 30 minutes.

2 Wash the prawns and carefully remove the shells, leaving the heads and tails intact. Pull the body from the squid and remove the quill. Cut the tentacles from the head and rinse under cold water. Pull off the outer skin and cut into 5mm/¼in rings. Cut the monkfish into 2.5cm/1in cubes.

3 Put the garlic, onions and fennel into a pan with the wine. Cover and simmer for 5 minutes until tender.

4 Add the monkfish, saffron, tomatoes and thyme in their liquid. Cover and cook for 3 minutes. Then add the prawns and squid. Cover and cook gently for 1–2 minutes (do not overcook or the squid will become tough).

5 Meanwhile, cook the pasta in a large pan of boiling, salted water until *al dente*. Drain thoroughly.

6 Divide the pasta among four serving dishes and top with the fish and shellfish sauce. Sprinkle with parsley and serve at once.

Black Pasta with Scallops

A stunning pasta dish using black tagliatelle.

INGREDIENTS

Serves 4

120ml/4fl oz/½ cup low-fat crème fraîche
10ml/2 tsp wholegrain mustard
2 garlic cloves, crushed
30–45ml/2–3 tbsp fresh lime juice
60ml/4 tbsp chopped fresh parsley
30ml/2 tbsp snipped chives
350g/12oz black tagliatelle
12 large scallops
60ml/4 tbsp white wine
150ml/¼ pint/⅔ cup fish stock
salt and ground black pepper
lime wedges and parsley sprigs, to garnish

1 To make the tartare sauce, mix the crème fraîche, mustard, garlic, lime juice, herbs and seasoning together in a bowl.

2 Cook the pasta in a large pan of boiling, salted water until *al dente*. Drain thoroughly.

3 Slice the scallops in half horizontally. Keep any coral whole. Put the white wine and fish stock into a saucepan and heat to simmering point. Add the scallops and cook very gently for 3–4 minutes (no longer or they will become tough).

4 Remove the scallops. Boil the wine and stock to reduce by half and add the green sauce to the pan. Heat gently to warm, replace the scallops and cook gently for 1 minute. Spoon over the pasta and garnish with lime wedges and sprigs of parsley.

Fried Singapore Noodles

Thai fishcakes vary in their size and their spiciness. They are available from Oriental supermarkets.

INGREDIENTS

Serves 4

175g/6oz rice noodles

60ml/4 tbsp vegetable oil

2.5ml/½ tsp salt

75g/3oz/¾ cup cooked prawns

175g/6oz cooked pork, cut
   into matchsticks

1 green pepper, seeded and cut
   into matchsticks

2.5ml/½ tsp sugar

10ml/2 tsp curry powder

75g/3oz Thai fishcakes

10ml/2 tsp dark soy sauce

1 Soak the rice noodles in water for about 10 minutes, drain well through a colander, then pat dry with kitchen paper.

2 Heat a wok, then add half the oil. When the oil is hot, add the noodles and salt and stir-fry for 2 minutes. Transfer to a warmed serving dish and keep warm.

3 Heat the remaining oil and add the prawns, pork, pepper, sugar, curry powder and remaining salt. Stir-fry for 1 minute.

4 Return the noodles to the pan and stir-fry with the Thai fishcakes for 2 minutes. Stir in the soy sauce and serve immediately.

Mixed Rice Noodles

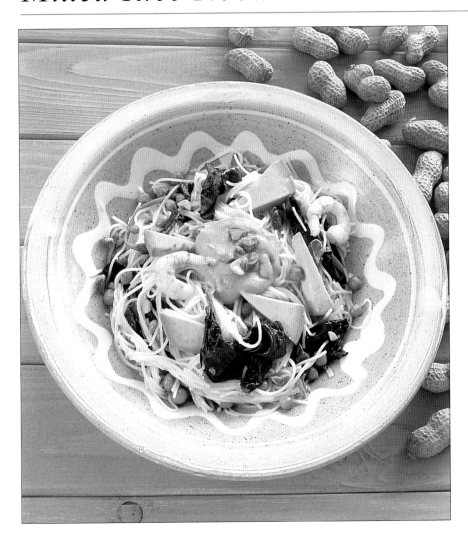

A delicious noodle dish made extra special by adding avocado and garnishing with prawns.

INGREDIENTS

Serves 4

15ml/1 tbsp sunflower oil

2.5cm/1in piece fresh root ginger, peeled and grated

2 garlic cloves, crushed

45ml/3 tbsp dark soy sauce

150ml/¼ pint/⅔ cup boiling water

225g/8oz/2 cups peas, thawed if frozen

450g/1lb rice noodles

450g/1lb fresh spinach, coarse stalks removed

30ml/2 tbsp smooth peanut butter

30ml/2 tbsp tahini paste

150ml/¼ pint/⅔ cup milk

1 ripe avocado, peeled and stoned

roasted peanuts and peeled prawns, to garnish

1 Heat a wok, then add the oil. When the oil is hot, stir-fry the ginger and garlic for 30 seconds. Add 15ml/1 tbsp of the soy sauce and the boiling water.

2 Add the peas and noodles, then cook for 3 minutes. Stir in the spinach. Remove the vegetables and noodles, drain well and keep warm.

3 Stir the smooth peanut butter, remaining soy sauce, tahini paste and milk together in the wok, and simmer for 1 minute.

4 Add the vegetables and noodles, slice in the avocado and toss together. Serve piled on individual plates. Spoon some sauce over each portion and garnish with peanuts and prawns.

Pasta with Prawns and Feta Cheese

This dish combines the richness of fresh prawns with the tartness of feta cheese. Goat's cheese could also be used, if preferred.

INGREDIENTS

Serves 4

450g/1lb raw prawns in the shell

6 spring onions

225g/8oz feta cheese

50g/2oz/4 tbsp butter

small bunch fresh chives

450g/1lb penne, garganelle or rigatoni

salt and ground black pepper

COOK'S TIP

If fresh prawns are not available, use well-thawed frozen, and add to the sauce at the last minute together with the spring onions.

1 Remove the heads from the prawns by twisting and pulling off. Peel the prawns and discard the shells.

2 On a nylon chopping board, chop the spring onions and the feta cheese using a sharp knife.

3 Melt the butter in a frying pan and stir in the prawns. When they turn pink, add the spring onions and cook gently over a low heat for about 1 minute.

4 Stir the feta cheese into the prawn mixture and season with black pepper.

5 Snip the chives into 2.5cm/1in lengths and stir half into the prawn mixture.

6 Cook the pasta in plenty of boiling salted water according to the instructions on the packet. Drain well, pile into a warmed serving dish and top with the sauce. Scatter with the remaining chives and serve.

Tagliatelle with Smoked Salmon

This is a pretty pasta dish with the light texture of the cucumber complementing the fish perfectly.

INGREDIENTS

Serves 4

350g/12oz tagliatelle
½ cucumber
75g/3oz/6 tbsp butter
grated rind of 1 orange
30ml/2 tbsp chopped fresh dill
300ml/½ pint/1¼ cups single cream
15ml/1 tbsp orange juice
115g/4oz smoked salmon, skinned
salt and ground black pepper

1 Cook the pasta in plenty of boiling salted water according to the instructions on the packet.

4 Melt the butter in a saucepan, add the orange rind and dill and stir well. Add the cucumber and cook gently for 2 minutes, stirring occasionally.

5 Add the cream and orange juice, and season to taste. Then simmer for 1 minute.

6 Meanwhile, cut the salmon into thin strips. Stir into the sauce and heat through.

7 Drain the pasta thoroughly and toss in the sauce until well coated. Serve immediately.

2 Using a sharp knife, cut the cucumber in half lengthways then, using a small spoon, scoop out the seeds and discard.

3 Turn the cucumber on the flat side and slice thinly.

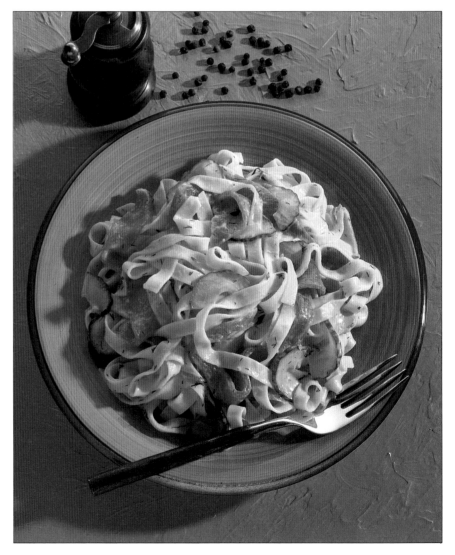

Mixed Summer Pasta

A pretty and colourful sauce with bags of flavour makes this a popular dish for the summer.

INGREDIENTS

Serves 4

115g/4oz French beans, cut into
    2.5cm/1in pieces
350g/12oz curly spaghetti (fusilli
    col buco)
30ml/2 tbsp olive oil
½ fennel bulb, sliced
1 bunch spring onions, sliced diagonally
115g/4oz yellow cherry tomatoes
115g/4oz red cherry tomatoes
30ml/2 tbsp chopped fresh dill
225g/8oz/2 cups peeled prawns
15ml/1 tbsp lemon juice
15ml/1 tbsp wholegrain mustard
60ml/4 tbsp soured cream
salt and ground black pepper
fresh dill sprigs, to garnish

1 Cook the beans in a saucepan of boiling salted water for about 5 minutes until tender. Drain through a colander.

2 Cook the pasta in plenty of boiling salted water, according to the instructions on the packet, until *al dente*.

3 Heat the oil in a frying pan and fry the sliced fennel and spring onions for about 5 minutes.

4 Stir in all the cherry tomatoes and fry for a further 5 minutes, stirring occasionally.

5 Add the dill and prawns and cook for 1 minute.

6 Stir in the lemon juice, wholegrain mustard, soured cream, seasoning and beans and simmer for 1 minute.

7 Drain the pasta and toss with the sauce. Serve immediately, garnished with fresh dill.

Spaghetti with Mussels

Mussels are popular in all the coastal regions of Italy, and are delicious with pasta. This simple dish is greatly improved by using the freshest mussels available.

Serves 4

900g/2lb fresh mussels, in the shell

75ml/5 tbsp olive oil

3 garlic cloves, finely chopped

60ml/4 tbsp chopped fresh parsley

60ml/4 tbsp white wine

400g/14oz spaghetti

salt and ground black pepper

1 Scrub the mussels well under cold running water, carefully cutting off the "beards" with a small sharp knife. Discard any that do not close when tapped sharply.

COOK'S TIP

Mussels should be firmly closed when fresh. If a mussel is slightly open, pinch it closed. If it remains closed on its own, it is alive. If it remains open, discard it. Fresh mussels should be consumed as soon as possible after being purchased. They may be kept in a bowl of cold water in the fridge.

2 Place the mussels with a cupful of water in a large saucepan over a moderate heat. As soon as they open, lift them out one by one with a slotted spoon.

3 When all the mussels have opened (discard any that do not), strain the liquid in the saucepan through a layer of kitchen paper to remove any grit, and reserve until needed.

4 Heat the oil in a large frying pan. Add the garlic and parsley, and cook for 2–3 minutes. Add the mussels, their cooking liquid and the wine. Cook over a moderate heat until heated through.

5 Add a generous amount of pepper to the sauce. Taste for seasoning; add salt if necessary.

6 Cook the pasta in plenty of boiling salted water until *al dente*. Drain, then tip it into the frying pan with the sauce, and stir well over a moderate heat for 3–4 minutes. Serve at once.

Spaghetti with Seafood Sauce

The Italian name for this tomato-based sauce is marinara.

INGREDIENTS

Serves 4

45ml/3 tbsp olive oil

1 onion, chopped

1 garlic clove, finely chopped

225g/8oz spaghetti

600ml/1 pint/2½ cups passata

15ml/1 tbsp tomato purée

5ml/1 tsp dried oregano

1 bay leaf

5ml/1 tsp sugar

115g/4oz/1 cup cooked peeled shrimps (rinsed well if canned)

115g/4oz/1 cup cooked peeled prawns

175g/6oz/1½ cups cooked clam or cockle meat (rinsed well if canned or bottled)

15ml/1 tbsp lemon juice

45ml/3 tbsp chopped fresh parsley

25g/1oz/2 tbsp butter

salt and ground black pepper

4 whole cooked prawns, to garnish

1 Heat the oil in a pan and add the onion and garlic. Fry over a moderate heat for 6–7 minutes, until the onions have softened.

2 Meanwhile, cook the spaghetti in a large saucepan of boiling salted water for 10–12 minutes until *al dente*.

3 Stir the passata, tomato purée, oregano, bay leaf and sugar into the onions and season well. Bring to the boil, then simmer for 2–3 minutes.

4 Add the shellfish, lemon juice and 30ml/2 tbsp of the parsley. Stir well, then cover and cook for 6–7 minutes.

5 Meanwhile, drain the spaghetti when it is ready and add the butter to the pan. Return the drained spaghetti to the pan and toss in the butter. Season well.

6 Divide the spaghetti among four warmed plates and top with the seafood sauce. Sprinkle with the remaining chopped parsley, garnish with whole prawns and serve immediately.

Pasta with Fresh Sardine Sauce

In this classic Sicilian dish, fresh sardines are combined with raisins and pine nuts.

INGREDIENTS

Serves 4

30g/1¼oz/3 tbsp sultanas

450g/1lb fresh sardines

90ml/6 tbsp breadcrumbs

1 small fennel bulb

90ml/6 tbsp olive oil

1 onion, very thinly sliced

30g/1¼oz/3 tbsp pine nuts

2.5ml/½ tsp fennel seeds

400g/14oz long hollow pasta, such as percatelli, zite or bucatini

salt and ground black pepper

1 Soak the sultanas in warm water for 15 minutes. Drain and pat dry.

2 Clean the sardines. Open each one out flat and remove the central bones and head. Wash well and shake dry. Sprinkle evenly with the breadcrumbs.

3 Coarsely chop the top fronds of fennel and reserve. Pull off a few outer leaves and wash. Fill a large saucepan with enough water to cook the pasta. Add the fennel leaves and bring to the boil.

4 Heat the oil in a large frying pan and sauté the onion lightly until soft. Remove to a side dish. Add the sardines, a few at a time, and cook over a moderate heat until golden on both sides, turning once. When all the sardines have been cooked, gently return them to the pan. Add the onion, and the sultanas, pine nuts and fennel seeds. Season with salt and pepper.

5 Take about 60ml/4 tbsp of the boiling water for the pasta, and add it to the sauce. Add salt to the boiling water, and cook the pasta until *al dente*. Drain, and remove the fennel leaves. Dress the pasta with the sauce. Divide among four individual serving plates, arranging several sardines on each. Sprinkle with the reserved chopped fennel tops and serve at once.

Spaghetti with Olives and Capers

This spicy sauce originated in the Naples area. It can be quickly assembled using a few store-cupboard ingredients.

INGREDIENTS

Serves 4

60ml/4 tbsp olive oil

2 garlic cloves, finely chopped

small piece of dried red chilli, crumbled

50g/2oz can anchovy fillets, chopped

350g/12oz tomatoes, fresh or
    canned, chopped

115g/4oz/1 cup stoned black olives

30ml/2 tbsp capers, rinsed

15ml/1 tbsp tomato purée

400g/14oz spaghetti

30ml/2 tbsp chopped fresh parsley

1 Heat the oil in a large frying pan. Add the garlic and the dried red chilli, and cook for 2–3 minutes until the garlic is just golden.

2 Add the chopped anchovies, and mash them into the garlic with a fork.

3 Add the fresh or canned tomatoes, olives, capers and tomato purée. Stir well and cook over a moderate heat.

4 Cook the spaghetti in plenty of boiling salted water until *al dente*. Drain well.

5 Turn the spaghetti into the sauce. Increase the heat and cook for 3–4 minutes, turning the pasta constantly. Sprinkle with parsley and serve at once.

Linguine with Clam and Tomato Sauce

There are two types of traditional Italian clam sauce for pasta: one with tomatoes, as here, and another version without.

INGREDIENTS

Serves 4

900g/2lb fresh clams in the shell, or 350g/12oz bottled clams, with their liquid

90ml/6 tbsp olive oil

1 garlic clove, crushed

400g/14oz tomatoes, fresh or canned, very finely chopped

350g/12oz linguine

60ml/4 tbsp chopped fresh parsley

salt and ground black pepper

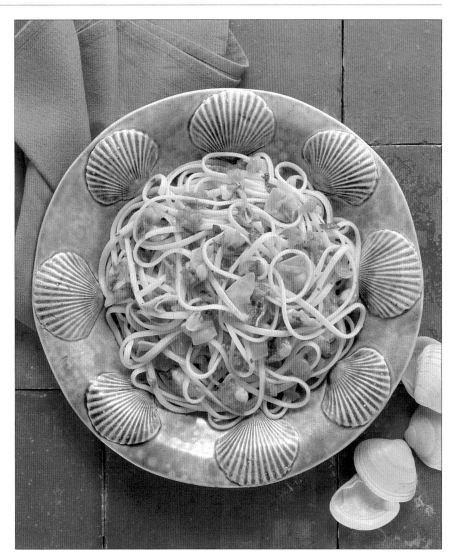

1 Scrub and rinse the clams well under cold running water. Place them in a large saucepan with a cupful of water, and heat until the clams begin to open. Lift each clam out as soon as it opens, and scoop it out of its shell using a small spoon. Place in a bowl.

2 If the clams are large, chop them into 2 or 3 pieces. Reserve any liquid from the shells in a separate bowl. When all the clams have opened (discard any that do not open), pour the cooking liquid into the juices from the clams, and strain them through a piece of kitchen paper to remove any sand. If using bottled clams, use the liquid from the jar.

3 Place the olive oil in a medium saucepan with the garlic. Cook over a moderate heat until golden.

4 Remove the garlic and discard. Add the chopped tomatoes to the oil, and pour in the clam liquid. Mix well and cook over a low to moderate heat until the sauce begins to dry out and thickens slightly.

5 Cook the pasta in plenty of boiling salted water until just *al dente*, following the instructions on the packet.

6 A minute or two before the pasta is cooked, stir the parsley and the clams into the tomato sauce, and increase the heat. Add pepper and taste for seasoning, adding salt if necessary. Drain the pasta and turn into a serving dish. Pour on the hot sauce and mix well before serving immediately.

MEALS IN MINUTES

Spaghetti with Herb Sauce

Herbs make a wonderfully aromatic sauce – the heat from the pasta releases their flavours.

INGREDIENTS

Serves 4

50g/2oz chopped fresh mixed herbs, such as parsley, basil and thyme

2 garlic cloves, crushed

60ml/4 tbsp pine nuts, toasted

150ml/¼ pint/⅔ cup olive oil

350g/12oz dried spaghetti

60ml/4 tbsp freshly grated Parmesan cheese

salt and ground black pepper

basil leaves, to garnish

1 Put the herbs, garlic and half the pine nuts into a blender or food processor. With the machine running slowly, add the oil and process to form a thick purée.

2 Cook the spaghetti in plenty of boiling salted water for about 8 minutes until *al dente*. Drain.

3 Transfer the herb purée to a large warmed serving dish, then add the spaghetti and Parmesan. Toss well to coat the pasta with the sauce. Sprinkle over the remaining pine nuts and the basil leaves and serve immediately.

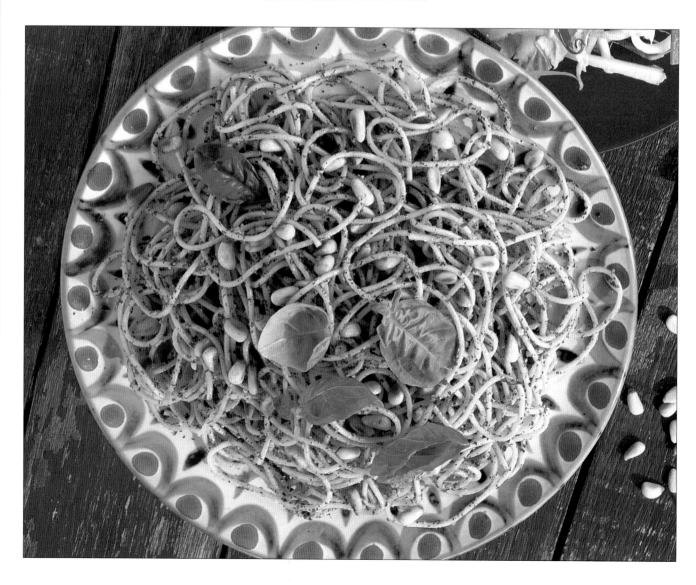

Beef Strips with Orange and Ginger

Stir-frying is one of the quickest ways to cook, but you do need to choose tender meat.

Serves 4

450g/1lb lean beef rump, fillet or sirloin, cut into thin strips
finely grated rind and juice of 1 orange
15ml/1 tbsp light soy sauce
5ml/1 tsp cornflour
2.5cm/1in piece fresh root ginger, finely chopped
10ml/2 tsp sesame oil
1 large carrot, cut into thin strips
2 spring onions, thinly sliced
rice noodles, to serve

1 Place the beef strips in a bowl and sprinkle over the orange rind and juice. Leave to marinate for at least 30 minutes.

2 Drain the liquid from the meat and reserve, then mix the meat with the soy sauce, cornflour and fresh root ginger.

3 Heat the oil in a wok or large frying pan and add the beef. Stir-fry for 1 minute until lightly coloured, then add the carrot and stir-fry for a further 2–3 minutes.

4 Stir in the spring onions and reserved liquid, then cook, stirring, until boiling and thickened. Serve the beef hot with rice noodles.

Fettuccine with Ham and Cream

Prosciutto is perfect for this rich and delicious dish, which makes a very elegant starter.

INGREDIENTS

Serves 4

115g/4oz prosciutto crudo or other
    unsmoked ham (raw or cooked)
50g/2oz/¼ cup butter
2 shallots, very finely chopped
150ml/¼ pint/⅔ cup double cream
350g/12oz fettucine
50g/2oz/½ cup grated Parmesan cheese
salt and ground black pepper
fresh parsley sprig, to garnish

1 Cut the fat from the ham and chop both lean and fat parts separately into small squares.

2 Melt the butter in a medium frying pan and add the shallots and the squares of ham fat. Cook until golden. Add the lean ham, and cook for a further 2 minutes. Season with black pepper. Stir in the cream, and keep warm over a low heat while the pasta is cooking.

3 Cook the pasta in plenty of boiling salted water until *al dente*. Drain, turn into a warmed serving dish and toss with the sauce. Stir in the cheese and serve immediately, garnished with a sprig of parsley.

Tagliatelle with Smoked Salmon

In Italy smoked salmon is imported and quite expensive. This elegant creamy sauce makes a little go a long way. Use a mixture of green and white pasta if you wish.

INGREDIENTS

Serves 4–5

175g/6oz smoked salmon slices or ends,
    fresh or frozen
300ml/½ pint/1¼ cups single cream
pinch of ground mace or grated nutmeg
350g/12oz green and white tagliatelle
salt and ground black pepper
45ml/3 tbsp snipped fresh chives,
    to garnish

1 Cut the salmon into thin strips about 5cm/2in long. Place in a bowl with the cream and the mace or nutmeg. Stir, cover and allow to stand for at least 2 hours in a cool place (not in the fridge).

2 Cook the pasta in plenty of boiling salted water until it is just *al dente*.

3 Meanwhile, gently warm the cream and salmon mixture in a small saucepan, without boiling.

4 Drain the pasta, pour the sauce over and mix well. Season to taste and garnish with the chives.

Twin Cities Meatballs

Serve these meatballs without gravy as drinks party nibbles.

INGREDIENTS

Serves 6

30ml/2 tbsp butter or margarine

½ small onion, minced

350g/12oz/2¼ cups minced beef

115g/4oz/1 cup minced veal

225g/8oz/2 cups minced pork

1 egg

40g/1½oz/½ cup mashed potatoes

30ml/2 tbsp finely chopped fresh dill
   or parsley

1 garlic clove, crushed

5ml/1 tsp salt

2.5ml/½ tsp black pepper

2.5ml/½ tsp ground allspice

1.5ml/¼ tsp grated nutmeg

40g/1½oz/¾ cup fresh breadcrumbs

175ml/6fl oz/¾ cup milk

25g/1oz/¼ cup plain flour plus
   15ml/1 tbsp extra

30ml/2 tbsp olive oil

175ml/6fl oz/¾ cup evaporated milk

buttered noodles, to serve

1 Melt the butter or margarine in a large frying pan. Add the onion and cook over a low heat until softened, about 8–10 minutes. Remove from the heat. Using a slotted spoon, transfer the onion to a large mixing bowl.

2 Add the beef, veal and pork, the egg, mashed potatoes, dill or parsley, garlic, salt, pepper, allspice and nutmeg to the bowl.

3 Put the breadcrumbs in a small bowl and add the milk. Stir until well moistened, then add to the other ingredients. Mix well.

4 Shape the mixture into balls about 2.5cm/1in in diameter. Roll them in 25g/1oz/¼ cup of the flour to coat all over.

5 Add the olive oil to the frying pan and heat over a medium heat. Add the meatballs and brown on all sides for 8–10 minutes. Shake the pan occasionally to roll the balls so they colour evenly. With a slotted spoon, remove the meatballs to a serving dish. Cover with foil and keep warm.

6 Stir the 15ml/1 tbsp of flour into the fat in the frying pan. Add the evaporated milk and mix in with a small whisk. Simmer for 3–4 minutes. Check the seasoning, and adjust if necessary.

7 Pour the gravy over the meatballs. Serve hot with buttered noodles.

Peasant Bolognese

A spicy version of a popular dish. Worcestershire sauce and chorizo sausages add an extra element to this perfect family standby.

INGREDIENTS

Serves 4

15ml/1 tbsp oil

225g/8oz/2 cups minced beef

1 onion, chopped

5ml/1 tsp chilli powder

15ml/1 tbsp Worcestershire sauce

25g/1oz/2 tbsp plain flour

150ml/¼ pint/⅔ cup beef stock

4 chorizo sausages

50g/2oz baby sweetcorn

200g/7oz can chopped tomatoes

15ml/1 tbsp chopped fresh basil

salt and ground black pepper

cooked spaghetti, to serve

fresh basil, to garnish

1 Heat the oil in a large pan and fry the minced beef for 5 minutes. Add the onion and chilli powder and cook for a further 3 minutes.

COOK'S TIP

Make up the Bolognese sauce and freeze in conveniently sized portions for up to two months.

2 Stir in the Worcestershire sauce and flour. Cook for 1 minute before pouring in the stock.

3 Slice the chirozo sausages and halve the corn lengthways.

4 Stir in the sausages, tomatoes, sweetcorn and chopped basil. Season well and bring to the boil. Reduce the heat and simmer for 30 minutes. Serve with spaghetti, garnished with fresh basil.

Tagliolini with Asparagus

Tagliolini are very thin egg noodles, more delicate in texture than spaghetti. They go well with this subtle cream sauce, flavoured with fresh asparagus.

INGREDIENTS

Serves 4

450g/1lb fresh asparagus
egg pasta sheets made with 2 eggs, or
   350g/12oz fresh tagliolini or other
   egg noodles
50g/2oz/¼ cup butter
3 spring onions, finely chopped
3–4 fresh mint or basil leaves,
   finely chopped
150ml/¼ pint/⅔ cup double cream
50g/2oz/½ cup freshly grated
   Parmesan cheese
salt and ground black pepper

1 Peel the asparagus by inserting a small sharp knife at the base of the stalks and pulling upwards towards the tips. Drop them into a pan of boiling water and boil until just tender, about 4–6 minutes.

2 Remove from the pan, reserving the cooking water. Cut the tips off, and then cut the stalks into 4cm/1½in pieces. Set aside.

3 Make the egg pasta sheets, if using, and fold and cut into thin noodles, or feed through the narrowest setting of a pasta-making machine. Open them out and dry for 5–10 minutes.

4 Melt the butter in a large frying pan. Add the spring onions and herbs, and cook for 3–4 minutes. Stir in the cream and asparagus, and heat gently, but do not boil. Season to taste.

5 Bring the asparagus cooking water back to the boil. Add salt. Drop the noodles in all at once. Cook until just tender (freshly made noodles will cook in about 30–60 seconds). Drain thoroughly through a colander.

6 Turn the pasta into the pan with the sauce, increase the heat slightly and mix well. Stir in the Parmesan cheese. Mix well and serve at once.

Spicy Beef

If you are hungry and only have a few minutes to spare for cooking, this colourful and healthy dish is an excellent choice.

INGREDIENTS

Serves 4

15ml/1 tbsp oil
450g/1lb/4 cups minced beef
2.5cm/1in piece fresh root ginger, sliced
5ml/1 tsp Chinese five-spice powder
1 red chilli, sliced
50g/2oz mange-touts
1 red pepper, seeded and chopped
1 carrot, sliced
115g/4oz beansprouts
15ml/1 tbsp sesame oil
cooked Chinese egg noodles, to serve

3 Add the mange-touts, the seeded and chopped red pepper and sliced carrot and cook for a further 3 minutes, stirring the mixture continuously.

4 Add the beansprouts and sesame oil and cook for a final 2 minutes. Serve immediately with Chinese egg noodles.

1 Heat the oil in a wok until almost smoking. Add the minced beef and cook for about 3 minutes, stirring all the time.

2 Add the ginger, Chinese five-spice powder and chilli. Cook for 1 minute.

Stir-fried Sweet and Sour Chicken

There are few cookery concepts that are better suited to today's busy lifestyle than the all-in-one stir-fry. This one has a wonderful South-east Asian influence.

INGREDIENTS

Serves 4

275g/10oz Chinese egg noodles

30ml/2 tbsp vegetable oil

3 spring onions, chopped

1 garlic clove, crushed

2.5cm/1in piece fresh root ginger, peeled
    and grated

5ml/1 tsp hot paprika

5ml/1 tsp ground coriander

3 boneless chicken breasts, sliced

115g/4oz/1 cup sugar-snap peas, topped
    and tailed

115g/4oz baby sweetcorn, halved

225g/8oz fresh beansprouts

15ml/1 tbsp cornflour

45ml/3 tbsp soy sauce

45ml/3 tbsp lemon juice

15ml/1 tbsp sugar

45ml/3 tbsp chopped fresh coriander or
    spring onion tops, to garnish

1 Bring a large saucepan of salted water to the boil. Add the noodles and cook according to the instructions on the packet. Drain, cover and keep warm.

2 Heat the oil in a wok. Add the spring onions and cook over a gentle heat. Mix in the next five ingredients, then stir-fry for about 3–4 minutes. Add the next three ingredients and steam briefly. Add the noodles.

3 Combine the cornflour, soy sauce, lemon juice and sugar in a small bowl. Add to the wok and simmer briefly to thicken. Serve garnished with chopped coriander or spring onion tops.

Pasta Spirals with Pepperoni and Tomato

A warming supper dish, perfect for a cold winter's night. All types of sausage are suitable, but if using raw sausages, add them with the onion to cook thoroughly.

INGREDIENTS

Serves 4

1 onion

1 red pepper

1 green pepper

30ml/2 tbsp olive oil, plus extra for
    tossing the pasta

800g/1¾ lb canned chopped tomatoes

30ml/2 tbsp tomato purée

10ml/2 tsp paprika

175g/6oz pepperoni or chorizo sausage

45ml/3 tbsp chopped fresh parsley

450g/1lb pasta spirals, such as fusilli

salt and ground black pepper

1 Chop the onion. Halve, core and seed the peppers. Cut the flesh into dice.

2 Heat the oil in a medium saucepan, add the onion and cook for 2–3 minutes until beginning to colour. Stir in the peppers, tomatoes, tomato purée and paprika, bring to the boil and simmer uncovered for about 15–20 minutes until reduced and thickened.

3 Slice the pepperoni or chorizo and stir into the sauce with 30ml/2 tbsp of the chopped parsley. Season to taste with salt and pepper.

4 While the sauce is simmering, cook the pasta in plenty of boiling salted water according to the instructions on the packet. Drain well. Toss the pasta with the remaining parsley in a little extra olive oil. Divide among four warmed bowls and top with sauce.

Farfalle with Prawns and Peas

A small amount of saffron in the sauce gives this dish a wonderful golden colour.

INGREDIENTS

Serves 4

45ml/3 tbsp olive oil

25g/1oz/2 tbsp butter

2 spring onions, chopped

350g/12oz/3 cups fresh or frozen peeled prawns

225g/8oz/1 cup frozen petit pois or peas, thawed

400g/14oz farfalle

250ml/8fl oz/1 cup dry white wine

a few saffron strands or pinch of powdered saffron

salt and ground black pepper

30ml/2 tbsp chopped fresh fennel or dill, to serve

1 Heat the oil and butter in a frying pan and sauté the spring onions lightly. Add the prawns and peas; cook for 2–3 minutes.

2 Cook the pasta in plenty of boiling salted water until just *al dente*.

3 Meanwhile, stir the wine and saffron into the prawn mixture.

4 Increase the heat and cook until the wine is reduced by about half. Add salt and pepper to taste. Cover and reduce the heat to low.

5 Drain the pasta and add it to the pan with the sauce. Stir over a high heat for 2–3 minutes, coating the pasta with the sauce. Sprinkle with the fresh herbs, and serve at once.

Short Pasta with Spring Vegetables

This colourful sauce makes the most of new crops of fresh, tender spring vegetables.

INGREDIENTS

Serves 6

1 or 2 small young carrots

2 spring onions

150g/5oz courgettes

2 tomatoes

75g/3oz/¾ cup shelled peas, fresh or frozen

75g/3oz fine green beans

1 yellow pepper

60ml/4 tbsp olive oil

25g/1oz/2 tbsp butter

1 garlic clove, finely chopped

5–6 fresh basil leaves, torn into pieces

500g/1¼lb short coloured or plain pasta, such as fusilli, penne or farfalle

salt and ground black pepper

freshly grated Parmesan cheese, to serve

1 Cut all the vegetables into small, bite-size pieces.

2 Heat the oil and butter in a large frying pan. Add the chopped vegetables, and cook over a moderate heat for 5–6 minutes, stirring occasionally. Add the garlic and the basil, and season with salt and pepper. Cover the pan and cook for a further 5–8 minutes, or until the vegetables are just tender.

3 Meanwhile, cook the pasta in plenty of boiling salted water until *al dente*. Before draining it, reserve a cupful of the pasta water.

4 Turn the pasta into the pan with the sauce, and mix well to distribute the vegetables. If the sauce seems too dry, add a few tablespoons of the reserved pasta water. Serve with the Parmesan handed round separately.

Tagliatelle with Prosciutto and Parmesan

This is a really simple dish, prepared in minutes from the best ingredients.

Serves 4

115g/4oz prosciutto

450g/1lb tagliatelle

75g/3oz/6 tbsp butter

50g/2oz/½ cup freshly grated
   Parmesan cheese

salt and ground black pepper

a few fresh sage leaves, to garnish

1 Cut the prosciutto into strips the same width as the tagliatelle. Cook the pasta in plenty of boiling salted water according to the instructions on the packet.

2 Meanwhile, melt the butter gently in a saucepan, stir in the prosciutto strips and heat through over a very gentle heat, being careful not to fry.

3 Drain the tagliatelle through a colander and pile into a warmed serving dish.

4 Sprinkle over all the Parmesan cheese and pour over the buttery prosciutto. Season well with black pepper and garnish with the sage leaves.

Capellini with Rocket and Mange-touts

A light but filling pasta dish with the added pepperiness of fresh rocket leaves.

INGREDIENTS

Serves 4

250g/9oz capellini or angel hair pasta

225g/8oz mange-touts

75g/3oz rocket leaves

50g/2oz/¼ cup pine nuts, roasted

30ml/2 tbsp finely grated Parmesan cheese (optional)

30ml/2 tbsp olive oil (optional)

1 Cook the capellini or angel-hair pasta in plenty of boiling salted water, according to the instructions on the packet, until just *al dente*.

2 Meanwhile, carefully top and tail the mange-touts, and discard any that are damaged.

3 As soon as the pasta is cooked, drop in the rocket and mange-touts. Drain immediately.

4 Toss the pasta with the roasted pine nuts, and Parmesan and olive oil if using. Serve at once.

Tagliatelle with Sun-dried Tomatoes

Choose plain sun-dried tomatoes for this sauce, instead of those preserved in oil, if you wish to reduce the fat content of the dish.

INGREDIENTS

Serves 4

1 garlic clove, crushed

1 celery stick, finely sliced

115g/4oz/1 cup sun-dried tomatoes, finely chopped

90ml/3½fl oz/scant ½ cup red wine

8 plum tomatoes

350g/12oz dried tagliatelle

salt and ground black pepper

3 Add the plum tomatoes to the saucepan and simmer for a further 5 minutes. Season to taste.

4 Meanwhile, cook the tagliatelle in plenty of boiling salted water for 8–10 minutes, or until *al dente*. Drain well. Toss with half the sauce and serve on warmed plates, with the remaining sauce.

1 Put the garlic, celery, sun-dried tomatoes and wine into a large saucepan. Gently cook for about 15 minutes.

2 Slash the bottoms of the plum tomatoes and plunge into a saucepan of boiling water for 1 minute, then into a saucepan of cold water. Slip off their skins. Halve, remove the seeds and cores and roughly chop the flesh.

Pasta Rapido with Parsley Pesto

Here is a fresh and lively sauce that will appeal to even the most jaded of appetites.

INGREDIENTS

Serves 4

450g/1lb dried pasta, any shape

75g/3oz/¾ cup whole almonds

50g/2oz/½ cup flaked almonds

25g/1oz/¼ cup freshly grated
Parmesan cheese

pinch of salt

For the sauce

40g/1½oz fresh parsley

2 garlic cloves, crushed

45ml/3 tbsp olive oil

45ml/3 tbsp lemon juice

5ml/1 tsp sugar

250ml/8fl oz/1 cup boiling water

2 For the sauce, chop the parsley finely in a blender or food processor. Add the whole almonds; reduce to a fine consistency. Add the garlic, oil, lemon juice, sugar and water. Combine to a sauce.

3 Drain the pasta and combine with half the sauce. (The remainder of the sauce will keep in a screw-top jar in the fridge for up to ten days.) Top with Parmesan and flaked almonds.

1 Cook the pasta in plenty of boiling salted water, according to the instructions on the packet, until *al dente*. Toast the whole and flaked almonds separately under a moderate grill until golden brown. Set the flaked almonds aside.

Pasta with Devilled Kidneys

Ask your butcher to prepare the kidneys for you if you prefer.

INGREDIENTS

Serves 4

8–10 lambs' kidneys

15ml/1 tbsp sunflower oil

25g/1oz/2 tbsp butter

10ml/2 tsp paprika

5–10ml/1–2 tsp mild grainy mustard

salt, to taste

chopped fresh parsley, to garnish

225g/8oz fresh pasta, to serve

1 Cut the kidneys in half and neatly cut out the white cores with scissors. Cut the kidneys again if very large.

2 Heat the oil and butter together. Add the kidneys and cook, turning frequently, for about 2 minutes. Blend the paprika and mustard together with a little salt and stir into the pan.

3 Continue cooking the kidneys, basting frequently, for about a further 3–4 minutes.

4 Cook the pasta for about 10–12 minutes, or according to the instructions on the packet. Serve the kidneys and their sauce, topped with the chopped fresh parsley, and accompanied by the pasta.

Golden-topped Pasta

When it comes to the children helping you to plan the menus, this is the sort of dish that always wins hands down. It is also perfect for "padding out" if you have to feed eight instead of four people.

INGREDIENTS

Serves 4–6

225g/8oz dried pasta shells or spirals

115g/4oz/⅔ cup chopped ham, beef or turkey

350g/12oz par-cooked mixed vegetables, such as carrots, cauliflower, beans, etc

a little oil

For the cheese sauce

25g/1oz/2 tbsp butter

25g/1oz/2 tbsp plain flour

300ml/½ pint/1¼ cups milk

175g/6oz/1½ cups grated Cheddar cheese

5–10ml/1–2 tsp mustard

salt and ground black pepper

1 Cook the pasta according to the instructions on the packet. Drain and place in a flameproof dish with the chopped meat, the vegetables and 5–10ml/1–2 tsp oil.

2 Melt the butter in a saucepan, stir in the flour and cook for 1 minute, stirring. Remove from the heat and gradually stir in the milk. Return to the heat, bring to the boil, stirring and cook for 2 minutes. Add half the cheese, the mustard and seasoning to taste.

3 Spoon the sauce over the meat and vegetables. Sprinkle with the rest of the cheese and grill quickly until golden and bubbling.

Oriental Vegetable Noodles

You could use Chinese egg noodles instead of tagliarini if you prefer.

INGREDIENTS

Serves 6

500g/1¼lb thin tagliarini

1 red onion

115g/4oz shiitake mushrooms

45ml/3 tbsp sesame oil

45ml/3 tbsp dark soy sauce

15ml/1 tbsp balsamic vinegar

10ml/2 tsp caster sugar

5ml/1 tsp salt

celery leaves, to garnish

1 Cook the tagliarini in plenty of boiling salted water according to the instructions on the packet until *al dente*.

2 Thinly slice the red onion and the shiitake mushrooms, using a sharp knife.

3 Heat a wok, then add 15ml/ 1 tbsp of the sesame oil. When the oil is hot, stir-fry the onion and mushrooms for about 2 minutes.

4 Drain the tagliarini, then add to the wok with the soy sauce, balsamic vinegar, sugar and salt. Stir-fry for 1 minute, then add the remaining sesame oil, and serve garnished with celery leaves.

Stir-fried Vegetables with Pasta

This is a colourful Chinese-style dish, easily prepared using pasta instead of Chinese noodles.

INGREDIENTS

Serves 4

1 carrot

175g/6oz small courgettes

175g/6oz runner or other green beans

175g/6oz baby sweetcorn

450g/1lb ribbon pasta, such as tagliatelle

salt, to taste

30ml/2 tbsp corn oil, plus extra for tossing the pasta

1cm/½in piece fresh root ginger, peeled and finely chopped

2 garlic cloves, finely chopped

90ml/6 tbsp yellow bean sauce

6 spring onions, sliced into 2.5cm/1in lengths

30ml/2 tbsp dry sherry

5ml/1 tsp sesame seeds, to garnish

1 Slice the carrot and courgettes diagonally into chunks. Slice the beans diagonally. Cut the baby sweetcorn diagonally in half.

2 Cook the pasta in plenty of boiling salted water according to the instructions on the packet. Drain, then rinse under hot water. Toss in a little corn oil.

3 Heat 30ml/2 tbsp oil until smoking in a wok or frying pan and add the ginger and garlic. Stir-fry for 30 seconds, then add the carrots, beans and courgettes.

4 Stir-fry for 3–4 minutes, then stir in the yellow bean sauce. Stir-fry for 2 minutes, add the spring onions, sherry and pasta and stir-fry for 1 minute or until piping hot. Sprinkle with sesame seeds and serve immediately.

Lasagne Rolls

Perhaps a more elegant presentation than ordinary lasagne, but just as tasty and popular. You will need to boil "no-need-to-cook" lasagne as it needs to be soft enough to roll!

INGREDIENTS

Serves 4

8-10 lasagne sheets

225g/8oz fresh leaf spinach, well washed

115g/4oz mushrooms, sliced

115g/4oz mozzarella cheese, thinly sliced

Lentil Bolognese (see below)

Béchamel Sauce

50g/2oz/scant ½ cup all-purpose flour

45ml/3 tbsp butter or margarine

600ml/1 pint/2½ cups milk

bay leaf

salt and ground black pepper

freshly grated nutmeg

freshly grated Parmesan or pecorino cheese, to serve

1 Cook the lasagne sheets according to instructions on the package, or until *al dente*. Drain and allow to cool.

2 Cook the spinach in the tiniest amount of water for 2 minutes then add the sliced mushrooms and cook for a further 2 minutes. Drain very well, pressing out all the excess liquor, and chop the spinach roughly.

3 Put all the béchamel ingredients into a saucepan and bring slowly to a boil, stirring until the sauce is thick and smooth. Simmer for 2 minutes with the bay leaf, then season well and stir in the grated nutmeg to taste.

4 Lay out the pasta sheets and spread with the béchamel sauce, spinach, mushrooms and mozzarella. Roll up each one and place in a large shallow casserole dish with the join face down in the dish.

5 Remove and discard the bay leaf and then pour the sauce over the pasta. Sprinkle the cheese and place under a hot grill to brown.

VARIATION

Needless to say, the fillings in this recipe could be any of your own choice. Another favourite is a lightly stir-fried mixture of colourful vegetables such as peppers, courgettes, aubergines and mushrooms, topped with a cheese béchamel as above, or with a fresh tomato sauce, which is especially good in summer.

Lentil Bolognese

A really useful sauce to serve with pasta, such as Lasagne Rolls (as above), as a crêpe stuffing or even as a protein-packed sauce for vegetables.

INGREDIENTS

Serves 6

1 onion

2 garlic cloves, crushed

2 carrots, coarsely grated

2 celery stalks, chopped

45ml/3 tbsp olive oil

150g/5oz/⅔ cup red lentils

14 oz can chopped tomatoes

45ml/3 tbsp tomato paste

475ml/16fl oz/2 cups stock

15ml/1 tbsp fresh marjoram, chopped, or 5ml/1 tsp dried marjoram

salt and ground black pepper

1 In a large saucepan, gently fry the onion, garlic, carrots and celery in the oil for about 5 minutes, until they are soft.

2 Add the lentils, tomatoes, tomato paste, stock and marjoram, and season to taste.

3 Bring the mixture to a boil, then partially cover with a lid and simmer for 20 minutes until thick and soft. Use the bolognese sauce as required.

Tagliatelle with Parma Ham and Asparagus

A stunning sauce, this is worth every effort to serve at a dinner party.

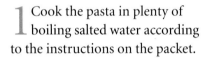

Serves 4

350g/12oz tagliatelle

25g/1oz/2 tbsp butter

15ml/1 tbsp olive oil

225g/8oz asparagus tips

1 garlic clove, chopped

115g/4oz Parma ham, sliced into strips

30ml/2 tbsp chopped fresh sage

150ml/¼ pint/⅔ cup single cream

115g/4oz/1 cup grated chive-and-onion
   double Gloucester cheese

115g/4oz/1 cup grated Gruyère cheese

salt and ground black pepper

fresh sage sprigs, to garnish

1 Cook the pasta in plenty of boiling salted water according to the instructions on the packet.

2 Melt the butter and oil in a frying pan and gently fry the asparagus tips for about 5 minutes, stirring occasionally, until they are almost tender.

3 Stir in the garlic and Parma ham and fry for 1 minute.

4 Stir in the chopped sage and fry for a further 1 minute.

5 Pour in the cream and bring the mixture to the boil.

6 Add the cheeses and simmer gently, stirring occasionally, until thoroughly melted. Season.

7 Drain the pasta thoroughly and toss with the sauce to coat. Serve immediately, garnished with fresh sage sprigs.

Curly Spaghetti with Walnut and Cream

A classic Italian dish with a strong, nutty flavour, this should be served with a delicately flavoured salad.

INGREDIENTS

Serves 4

350g/12oz curly spaghetti (fusilli col buco)
50g/2oz/½ cup walnut pieces
25g/1oz/2 tbsp butter
300ml/½ pint/1¼ cups milk
50g/2oz/1 cup fresh breadcrumbs
25g/1oz/2 tbsp freshly grated Parmesan cheese
pinch of freshly grated nutmeg
salt and ground black pepper
fresh rosemary sprigs, to garnish

1 Cook the pasta in plenty of boiling salted water according to the instructions on the packet. Meanwhile, preheat the grill.

2 Spread the walnuts evenly over the grill pan. Grill for about 5 minutes, turning occasionally until evenly toasted.

3 Remove the walnuts from the heat, place in a clean dish towel and rub away the skins. Roughly chop the nuts.

4 Heat the butter and milk in a saucepan until the butter is completely melted.

5 Stir in the breadcrumbs and nuts and heat gently for 2 minutes, stirring constantly until thickened.

6 Add the Parmesan cheese, nutmeg and seasoning to taste.

7 Drain the pasta thoroughly through a colander and toss in the sauce. Serve immediately, garnished with fresh sprigs of rosemary.

Cannelloni al Forno

A lighter alternative to the usual beef-filled, béchamel-coated version. Fill with ricotta cheese, onion and mushroom for a vegetarian version.

INGREDIENTS

Serves 4–6

450g/1lb skinless, boneless chicken
  breast, cooked
225g/8oz mushrooms
2 garlic cloves, crushed
30ml/2 tbsp chopped fresh parsley
15ml/1 tbsp chopped fresh tarragon
1 egg, beaten
freshly squeezed lemon juice
12–18 cannelloni tubes
1 quantity Napoletana Sauce
50g/2oz/½ cup freshly grated
  Parmesan cheese
salt and ground black pepper
fresh parsley sprig, to garnish

1 Preheat the oven to 200°C/ 400°F/Gas 6. Place the chicken in a blender or food processor and process until finely minced. Transfer to a bowl.

2 Place the mushrooms, garlic, parsley and tarragon in the blender or food processor and process until finely minced.

3 Beat the mushroom mixture into the chicken with the egg, salt and ground black pepper and lemon juice to taste.

4 If necessary, cook the cannelloni in plenty of salted boiling water according to the instructions on the packet. Drain well and pat dry on a clean dish towel.

5 Place the filling in a piping bag fitted with a large plain nozzle. Use to fill each tube of cannelloni.

6 Lay the filled cannelloni tightly together in a single layer in a buttered shallow ovenproof dish. Spoon over the tomato sauce and sprinkle with Parmesan cheese. Bake in the oven for 30 minutes or until brown and bubbling. Serve the cannelloni garnished with a sprig of parsley.

Magnificent Marrow

At autumn time, marrows – with their wonderful green and cream stripes – look so attractive and tempting. They make delicious, inexpensive main courses, just right for a satisfying family meal.

INGREDIENTS

Serves 4–6

250g/9oz pasta shells
1.5–1.75kg/3–4½lb marrow
1 onion, chopped
1 pepper, seeded and chopped
15ml/1 tbsp fresh root ginger, grated
2 garlic cloves, crushed
45ml/3 tbsp sunflower oil
4 large tomatoes, skinned and chopped
50g/2oz/½ cup pine nuts
15ml/1 tbsp chopped fresh basil
salt and ground black pepper
grated cheese, to serve (optional)

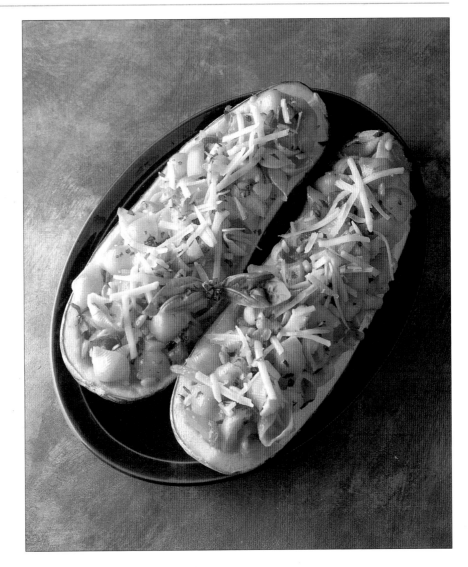

1 Preheat the oven to 190°C/ 375°F/Gas 5. Cook the pasta in plenty of boiling salted water according to the instructions on the packet, slightly overcooking it so it is just a little soft. Drain well and reserve.

2 Cut the marrow in half lengthways and scoop out and discard the seeds. Use a small sharp knife and tablespoon to scoop out the marrow flesh. Chop the flesh roughly.

3 Gently fry the onion, pepper, ginger and garlic in the oil for 5 minutes then add the marrow flesh, tomatoes and seasoning. Cover and cook for 10–12 minutes until the vegetables are soft.

4 Add the pasta, pine nuts and basil to the pan, stir well and set aside until required.

5 Meanwhile, place the marrow halves in a roasting tin, season lightly and pour a little water around the marrow, taking care it does not spill inside. Cover with foil and bake for 15 minutes.

6 Remove the foil, discard the water and fill the shells with the vegetable mixture. Cover with foil and return to the oven for a further 20–25 minutes.

7 Top with cheese, if using. To serve, scoop out of the "shell" or cut into sections.

Tagliatelle with Chicken and Herb Sauce

Serve this delicious dish with its wine-flavoured sauce and a fresh green salad.

INGREDIENTS

Serves 4

30ml/2 tbsp olive oil

1 red onion, cut into wedges

350g/12oz tagliatelle

1 garlic clove, chopped

350g/12oz chicken, diced

300ml/½ pint/1¼ cups dry vermouth

45ml/3 tbsp chopped fresh mixed herbs

150ml/¼ pint/⅔ cup fromage frais

salt and ground black pepper

shredded fresh mint, to garnish

1 Heat the oil in a large frying pan and fry the red onion for 10 minutes until softened and the layers have separated.

2 Cook the pasta in plenty of boiling salted water according to the instructions on the packet.

3 Add the garlic and chicken to the frying pan and fry for 10 minutes, stirring occasionally, until the chicken is browned all over and cooked through.

4 Pour in the vermouth, bring to boiling point and boil rapidly until reduced by about half.

5 Stir in the herbs, fromage frais and seasoning and heat through gently, but do not boil.

6 Drain the pasta thoroughly and toss with the sauce to coat. Serve immediately, garnished with shredded fresh mint.

Penne with Sausage and Parmesan Sauce

Spicy sausage tossed in a cheesy tomato sauce is delicious served on a bed of cooked pasta.

INGREDIENTS

Serves 4

350g/12oz penne
450g/1lb ripe tomatoes
30ml/2 tbsp olive oil
225g/8oz chorizo sausage,
    diagonally sliced
1 garlic clove, chopped
30ml/2 tbsp chopped fresh flat leaf parsley
grated rind of 1 lemon
50g/2oz/½ cup freshly grated
    Parmesan cheese
salt and ground black pepper
finely chopped fresh flat leaf parsley,
    to garnish

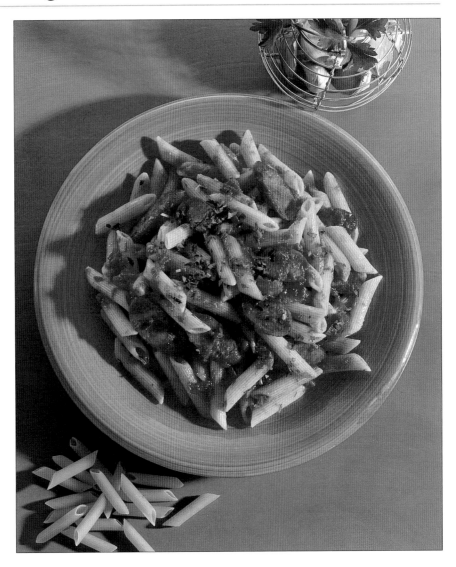

1 Cook the pasta in plenty of boiling salted water according to the instructions on the packet.

2 Slash the bottoms of the tomatoes with a knife, making a cross. Place in a large bowl, cover with boiling water and leave to stand for 45 seconds. Plunge into cold water for 30 seconds, then peel off the skins and roughly chop the flesh.

3 Heat the oil in a frying pan and fry the sliced chorizo sausage for 5 minutes, stirring from time to time, until browned.

4 Add the chopped tomatoes, garlic, parsley and grated lemon rind. Heat through gently, stirring, for 1 minute.

5 Add the grated Parmesan cheese and season to taste.

6 Drain the pasta well through a colander and toss it with the sauce to coat. Serve immediately, garnished with finely chopped fresh flat leaf parsley.

Short Pasta with Cauliflower

This is a pasta version of cauliflower cheese. The cauliflower water is used to cook the pasta.

INGREDIENTS

Serves 6

1 cauliflower

475ml/16fl oz/2 cups milk

1 bay leaf

50g/2oz/¼ cup butter

50g/2oz/½ cup flour

75g/3oz/¾ cup freshly grated Parmesan
   or Cheddar cheese

500g/1¼lb pennoni rigati or other
   short pasta

salt and ground black pepper

1 Bring a large pan of water to the boil. Wash the cauliflower well, and separate it into florets. Boil the florets until they are just tender, about 8–10 minutes.

Remove from the pan with a slotted spoon. Chop the cauliflower into bite-size pieces and set aside. Do not discard the cooking water in the pan.

2 Make a béchamel sauce by gently heating the milk with the bay leaf in a small saucepan. Do not let it boil. Melt the butter in a medium heavy-based saucepan. Add the flour, and mix in well with a wire whisk ensuring there are no lumps. Cook for 2–3 minutes, but do not let the butter burn.

3 Strain the hot milk into the flour and butter mixture all at once, and mix smoothly with the wire whisk.

4 Bring the sauce to the boil, stirring constantly, and cook for a further 4-5 minutes. Season to taste. Add the cheese, and stir over a low heat until melted. Stir in the cauliflower. Keep warm.

5 Bring the cauliflower cooking water back to the boil. Add salt, stir in the pasta and cook until *al dente*. Drain, and tip the pasta into a warmed serving dish. Pour over the sauce. Mix well, and serve at once.

Spaghetti with Bacon and Onion

This easy sauce is quickly made from ingredients that are almost always at hand.

INGREDIENTS

Serves 6

30ml/2 tbsp olive oil or lard

115g/4oz unsmoked streaky bacon, cut
   into matchsticks

1 small onion, finely chopped

120ml/4fl oz/½ cup dry white wine

450g/1lb tomatoes, fresh or
   canned, chopped

1.5ml/¼ tsp thyme leaves

600g/1lb 6oz spaghetti

salt and ground black pepper

freshly grated Parmesan cheese, to serve

1 In a medium frying pan, heat the oil or lard. Add the bacon and onion, and cook over a low to moderate heat until the onion is golden and the bacon has rendered its fat and is beginning to brown, about 8–10 minutes.

2 Add the wine to the bacon and onion, increase the heat and cook rapidly until the liquid boils off. Add the tomatoes, thyme, salt and pepper. Cover and cook over a moderate heat for 10–15 minutes.

3 Cook the pasta in plenty of boiling salted water until *al dente*. Drain, toss with the sauce and hand round the grated Parmesan cheese separately.

Pasta Bows with Fennel and Walnut

A scrumptious blend of walnuts and crisp steamed fennel.

INGREDIENTS

Serves 4

75g/3oz/½ cup walnuts, roughly chopped

1 garlic clove, chopped

25g/1oz fresh flat-leaf parsley, picked from the stalks

115g/4oz/½ cup ricotta cheese

450g/1lb pasta bows

450g/1lb fennel bulbs

chopped walnuts, to garnish

1 Place the chopped walnuts, garlic and parsley in a food processor. Pulse until roughly chopped. Transfer to a bowl and stir in the ricotta cheese.

2 Cook the pasta following the instructions on the packet until *al dente*. Drain thoroughly.

3 Slice the fennel thinly and steam for 4–5 minutes until just tender but still crisp.

4 Return the pasta to the pan and add the walnut mixture and the fennel. Toss well and sprinkle with the chopped walnuts to garnish. Serve immediately.

Pasta Tossed with Grilled Vegetables

A hearty dish to be eaten with crusty bread and washed down with a robust red wine. Try barbecuing the vegetables for a really smoky flavour.

INGREDIENTS

Serves 4

1 aubergine

2 courgettes

1 red pepper

3 garlic cloves, unpeeled

about 150ml/¼ pint/⅔ cup good olive oil

450g/1lb ribbon pasta pappardelle

salt and ground black pepper

a few sprigs fresh thyme, to garnish

1 Preheat the grill. With a sharp knife, slice the aubergine and courgettes lengthways.

2 Halve the pepper, cut out the stalk and white pith and scrape out the seeds. Slice the pepper lengthways into eight pieces.

3 Line a grill pan with foil and arrange the vegetables and unpeeled garlic in a single layer over the foil. Brush liberally with oil and season with salt and ground black pepper.

4 Grill until slightly charred, turning once. If necessary, cook the vegetables in two batches.

5 Cool the garlic, remove the charred skins and halve. Toss the vegetables with olive oil and keep warm.

6 Meanwhile cook the pasta in plenty of boiling salted water according to the instructions on the packet. Drain well and toss with the grilled vegetables. Serve immediately garnished with sprigs of fresh thyme.

Spinach and Ricotta Conchiglie

Large pasta shells are designed to hold a variety of delicious stuffings. Few are more pleasing than this mixture of spinach and ricotta.

INGREDIENTS

Serves 4

350g/12oz large conchiglie

450ml/¾ pint/1¾ cups passata or
    tomato pulp

275g/10oz frozen chopped
    spinach, thawed

50g/2oz crustless white bread, crumbled

120ml/4fl oz/½ cup milk

45ml/3 tbsp olive oil

250g/9oz ricotta cheese

pinch of grated nutmeg

1 garlic clove, crushed

15ml/1 tsbp olive oil

2.5ml/½ tsp black olive paste (optional)

25g/1oz/2 tbsp pine nuts

Parmesan cheese, for sprinkling

salt and ground black pepper

1 Cook the pasta in plenty of boiling salted water according to the instructions on the packet. Rinse under cold water, drain and reserve until needed.

2 Pour the passata or tomato pulp into a nylon sieve over a bowl and strain to thicken. Place the spinach in another sieve and press out any excess liquid with the back of a spoon.

3 Place the bread, milk and oil in a blender or food processor and process to combine. Add the spinach and ricotta cheese and season with salt, pepper and grated nutmeg.

4 Combine the passata or tomato pulp with the garlic, olive oil and olive paste, if using. Spread the sauce evenly over the base of an ovenproof dish.

5 Spoon the spinach mixture into a piping bag fitted with a large plain nozzle and fill the pasta shapes (alternatively fill with a spoon). Arrange the pasta shapes over the sauce.

6 Preheat the grill to a moderate heat. Heat the pasta through in the microwave on a high power for 4 minutes. Scatter with Parmesan cheese and pine nuts, and finish under the grill to brown the cheese until bubbling.

SALADS
& STARTERS

Wholemeal Pasta Salad

This substantial vegetarian salad is easily assembled from any combination of seasonal vegetables. Use raw or lightly blanched vegetables, or a mixture of both.

INGREDIENTS

Serves 8

450g/1lb short wholemeal pasta, such as fusilli or penne
45ml/3 tbsp olive oil
2 carrots
1 small bunch broccoli
175g/6oz/1½ cups shelled peas, fresh or frozen
1 red or yellow pepper
2 celery sticks
4 spring onions
1 large tomato
75g/3oz/¾ cup stoned olives
115g/4oz/1 cup diced Cheddar or mozzarella cheese or a combination of both
salt and ground black pepper

For the dressing
45ml/3 tbsp white wine or balsamic vinegar
60ml/4 tbsp olive oil
15ml/1 tbsp Dijon mustard
15ml/1 tbsp sesame seeds
10ml/2 tsp chopped mixed fresh herbs, such as parsley, thyme and basil

1 Cook the pasta in plenty of boiling salted water until *al dente*. Drain, and rinse under cold water to stop the cooking. Drain well and turn into a large bowl. Toss with 45ml/3 tbsp of the olive oil and set aside. Allow the pasta to cool completely.

2 Lightly blanch the carrots, broccoli and peas in a large pan of boiling water. Refresh under cold water. Drain well.

3 Chop the carrots and broccoli into bite-size pieces and add to the pasta with the peas. Slice the pepper, celery, spring onions and tomato into small pieces. Add them to the salad with the olives.

4 Make the dressing in a small bowl by combining the vinegar with the oil and mustard. Stir in the sesame seeds and herbs. Mix the dressing into the salad. Taste for seasoning, adding salt, pepper or more olive oil and vinegar if necessary. Stir in the cheese, then allow the salad to stand for about 15 minutes before serving.

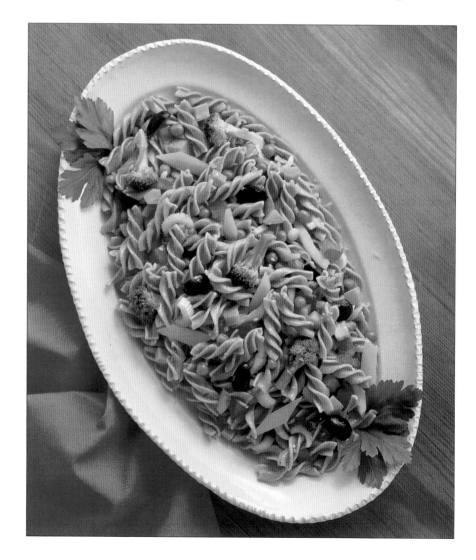

Pasta Salad with Olives

This delicious salad combines all the flavours of the Mediterranean. It is an excellent way of serving pasta and is particularly suitable for a hot summer's day.

INGREDIENTS

Serves 6

450g/1lb short pasta, such as medium
    shells, farfalle or penne
60ml/4 tbsp extra virgin olive oil
10 sun-dried tomatoes, thinly sliced
30ml/2 tbsp capers, in brine or salted
115g/4oz/1 cup stoned black olives
2 garlic cloves, finely chopped
45ml/3 tbsp balsamic vinegar
45ml/3 tbsp chopped fresh parsley
salt and ground black pepper

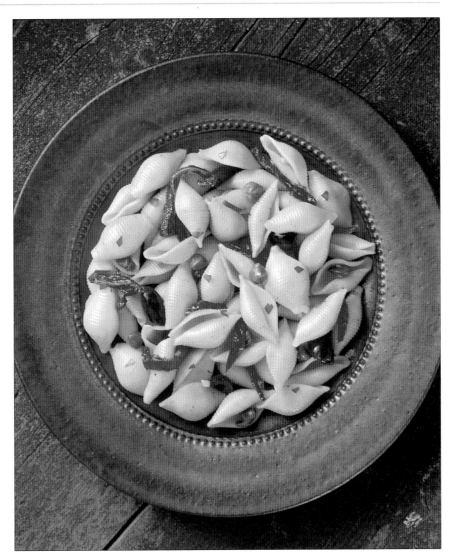

1 Cook the pasta in plenty of boiling salted water until *al dente*. Drain and rinse under cold water to stop the cooking. Drain well and turn into a large bowl. Toss with the olive oil and set aside until required.

2 Soak the tomatoes in a bowl of hot water for 10 minutes. Do not discard the water. Rinse the capers well. If they have been preserved in salt, soak them in a little hot water for 10 minutes. Rinse again.

3 Combine the olives, tomatoes, capers, garlic and vinegar in a small bowl. Season with salt and ground black pepper.

4 Stir the olive mixture into the cooked pasta and toss well. Add 30–45ml/2–3 tbsp of the tomato soaking water if the salad seems too dry. Toss with the parsley and allow to stand for 15 minutes before serving.

Artichoke Pasta Salad

Broccoli and black olives add colour to this delicious salad.

INGREDIENTS

Serves 4

105ml/7 tbsp olive oil

1 red pepper, quartered, seeded, and
   thinly sliced

1 onion, halved and thinly sliced

5ml/1 tsp dried thyme

45ml/3 tbsp sherry vinegar

450g/1lb pasta shapes, such as penne
   or fusilli

2 x 175g/6oz jars marinated artichoke
   hearts, drained and thinly sliced

150g/5oz cooked broccoli, chopped

20–25 salt-cured black olives, stoned
   and chopped

30ml/2 tbsp chopped fresh parsley

salt and ground black pepper

1 Heat 30ml/2 tbsp of the olive oil in a non-stick frying pan. Add the red pepper and onion and cook over a low heat until just soft, about 8–10 minutes, stirring from time to time.

2 Stir in the thyme, 1.5ml/¼ tsp salt and the vinegar. Cook, stirring, for a further 30 seconds, then set aside.

3 Cook the pasta in plenty of boiling salted water according to the instructions on the packet until *al dente*. Drain, rinse with hot water, then drain again. Transfer to a large bowl. Add 30ml/2 tbsp of the oil and toss well to coat thoroughly.

4 Add the artichokes, broccoli, olives, parsley, onion mixture and remaining oil to the pasta. Season with salt and pepper. Stir to blend. Leave to stand for at least 1 hour before serving or chill overnight. Serve the salad at room temperature.

Smoked Trout Pasta Salad

Bulb fennel gives this salad a lovely aniseed flavour.

Serves 6

15ml/1 tbsp butter

115g/4oz minced bulb fennel

6 spring onions, 2 minced and
    4 thinly sliced

225g/8oz skinless smoked trout
    fillets, flaked

45ml/3 tbsp chopped fresh dill

115g/4oz/½ cup mayonnaise

10ml/2 tsp fresh lemon juice

30ml/2 tbsp whipping cream

450g/1lb small pasta shapes, such as shells

salt and ground black pepper

fresh dill sprigs, to garnish

2 Add the sliced spring onions, trout, dill, mayonnaise, lemon juice and cream. Mix gently until well blended.

3 Cook the pasta in plenty of boiling salted water according to the instructions on the packet until *al dente*. Drain thoroughly and leave to cool.

4 Add the pasta to the vegetable and trout mixture and toss to coat evenly. Taste for seasoning and adjust if necessary. Serve the salad lightly chilled or at room temperature, garnished with dill.

1 Melt the butter in a small non-stick frying pan. Add the fennel and minced spring onions and season lightly with salt and black pepper. Cook over a medium heat for 3–5 minutes, or until just softened. Transfer to a large bowl and leave to cool slightly.

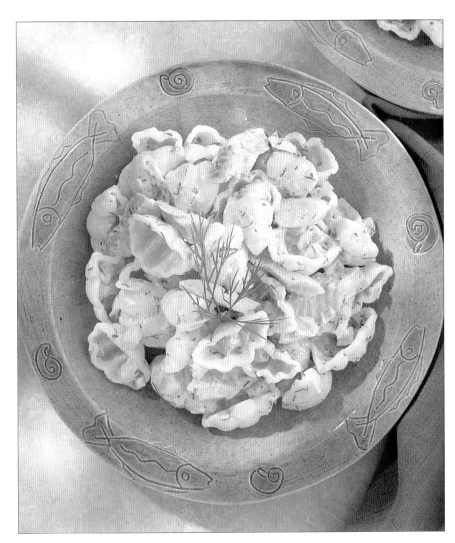

Tuna Pasta Salad

This easy pasta salad uses canned beans and tuna for a quick main course dish.

INGREDIENTS

Serves 6–8

450g/1lb short pasta, such as macaroni or farfalle

60ml/4 tbsp olive oil

2 x 200g/7oz cans tuna, drained and flaked

2 x 400g/14oz cans cannellini or borlotti beans, rinsed and drained

1 small red onion

2 celery sticks

juice of 1 lemon

30ml/2 tbsp chopped fresh parsley

salt and ground black pepper

1 Cook the pasta in plenty of boiling salted water until a*l dente*. Drain, and rinse under cold water to stop the cooking. Drain well and turn into a large bowl. Toss with the olive oil and set aside. Allow to cool completely.

2 Mix the flaked tuna and the beans into the cooked pasta. Slice the onion and celery very thinly and add them to the pasta.

3 Combine the lemon juice with the parsley. Mix into the other ingredients. Season with salt and pepper. Allow the salad to stand for at least 1 hour before serving.

Chicken Pasta Salad

This salad uses leftover chicken from a roast or a cold poached chicken breast if you prefer.

INGREDIENTS

Serves 4

350g/12oz short pasta, such as mezze, rigatoni, fusilli or penne

45ml/3 tbsp olive oil

225g/8oz cold cooked chicken

2 small red and yellow peppers

50g/2oz/½ cup stoned green olives

4 spring onions, chopped

45ml/3 tbsp mayonnaise

5ml/1 tsp Worcestershire sauce

15ml/1 tbsp white wine vinegar

salt and ground black pepper

a few fresh basil leaves, to garnish

1 Cook the pasta in plenty of boiling salted water until *al dente*. Drain, and rinse under cold water to stop the cooking. Drain well and turn into a large bowl. Toss with the olive oil and set aside. Allow to cool completely.

2 Cut the chicken into bite-size pieces, removing any bones. Cut the peppers into small pieces.

3 Combine all the ingredients except the pasta in a medium bowl. Taste for seasoning, then mix into the pasta. Serve well chilled, garnished with basil leaves.

Pasta, Asparagus and Potato Salad

A meal in itself, this is a real treat when made with fresh asparagus just in season.

INGREDIENTS

Serves 4

225g/8oz wholemeal pasta shapes
60ml/4 tbsp extra virgin olive oil
350g/12oz baby new potatoes
225g/8oz fresh asparagus
115g/4oz Parmesan cheese
salt and ground black pepper

1 Cook the pasta in boiling salted water according to the instructions on the packet. Drain well and toss with the olive oil and salt and pepper while still warm.

2 Wash the potatoes and cook in boiling salted water for about 12–15 minutes or until tender. Drain and toss with the pasta.

3 Trim any woody ends off the asparagus and halve the stalks if very long. Blanch in boiling salted water for 6 minutes until bright green and still crunchy. Drain, refresh in cold water and allow to cool. Drain and pat dry.

4 Toss the asparagus with the potatoes and pasta, season and transfer to a shallow bowl. Using a rotary vegetable peeler, shave over the Parmesan. Serve immediately.

Roquefort and Walnut Pasta Salad

This is a simple earthy salad, relying totally on the quality of the ingredients. There is no real substitute for Roquefort – a blue-veined ewe's-milk cheese which comes from south-western France.

INGREDIENTS

Serves 4

225g/8oz pasta shapes

mixed salad leaves, such as rocket, curly
    endive, lamb's lettuce, baby spinach,
    radicchio, etc

30ml/2 tbsp walnut oil

60ml/4 tbsp sunflower oil

30ml/2 tbsp red wine vinegar or
    sherry vinegar

225g/8oz Roquefort cheese,
    roughly crumbled

115g/4oz/1 cup walnut halves

salt and ground black pepper

1 Cook the pasta in plenty of boiling salted water according to the instructions on the packet. Drain well and cool. Wash and dry the salad leaves and place them in a large bowl.

COOK'S TIP

Try toasting the walnuts under the grill for a couple of minutes to release the flavour.

2 Whisk together the walnut oil, sunflower oil, vinegar and salt and pepper to taste.

3 Pile the pasta in the centre of the leaves, scatter over the crumbled Roquefort and pour over the dressing.

4 Scatter over the walnuts. Toss just before serving.

Pasta and Beetroot Salad

Colour is vital at a party table, and this salad is certainly eye-catching. Prepare the egg and avocado at the last moment to avoid discoloration.

INGREDIENTS

Serves 8

2 uncooked beetroots, scrubbed

225g/8oz pasta shells or twists

45ml/3 tbsp vinaigrette dressing

2 celery sticks, thinly sliced

3 spring onions, sliced

75g/3oz/¾ cup walnuts or hazelnuts, roughly chopped

1 eating apple, cored, halved and sliced

salt and ground black pepper

For the dressing

60ml/4 tbsp mayonnaise

45ml/3 tbsp natural yogurt or fromage frais

30ml/2 tbsp milk

10ml/2 tsp creamed horseradish

To serve

curly lettuce leaves

3 eggs, hard-boiled and chopped

2 ripe avocados

1 box salad cress

1 Boil the beetroots, without peeling, in lightly salted water until they are just tender, about 1 hour. Drain, cool, then peel and chop. Set aside.

2 Cook the pasta in plenty of boiled salted water according to the instructions on the packet. Drain, toss in the vinaigrette and season well. Leave to cool then mix with the beetroot, celery, onions, nuts and apple in a bowl.

3 Stir all the dressing ingredients together and then mix into the pasta. Chill well.

4 To serve, line a salad bowl with the lettuce and spoon in the salad. Scatter over the chopped egg. Peel and slice the avocados and arrange them on top then sprinkle over the cress.

Warm Pasta Salad with Ham and Egg

*In the summer months when the
weather is hot, try serving your
pasta* calda, *as a warm salad. Here
it is served with ham, eggs and
asparagus. A mustard dressing made
from the thick part of asparagus
provides a rich accompaniment.*

INGREDIENTS

Serves 4

450g/1lb asparagus

salt, to taste

450g/1lb dried tagliatelle

225g/8oz sliced cooked ham, 5mm/¼in
thick, cut into fingers

2 eggs, hard-boiled and sliced

50g/2oz Parmesan cheese, shaved

For the dressing

50g/2oz cooked potato

75g/5 tbsp olive oil, preferably Sicilian

15ml/1 tbsp lemon juice

10ml/2 tsp Dijon mustard

120ml/4fl oz/½ cup vegetable stock

1 Bring a saucepan of salted
water to the boil. Trim and
discard the tough woody parts of
the asparagus. Cut the asparagus in
half and boil the thicker halves for
12 minutes. After 6 minutes throw
in the tips. Refresh under cold
water until warm, then drain.

2 Finely chop 150g/5oz of the
asparagus middle section. Place
in a blender or food processor with
the dressing ingredients and
process until smooth. Season to
taste with salt and pepper.

3 Cook the pasta in plenty of
boiling salted water according
to the instructions on the packet.
Refresh under cold water until
warm, then drain. Dress with the
asparagus sauce and turn out on to
four pasta plates. Top the pasta
with the ham, hard-boiled eggs
and asparagus tips. Finish with
Parmesan cheese shavings.

Avocado, Tomato and Mozzarella Salad

This salad is made from ingredients representing the colours of the Italian flag – a sunny cheerful dish!

Serves 4

175g/6oz farfalle
6 ripe red tomatoes
225g/8oz mozzarella cheese
1 large ripe avocado
30ml/2 tbsp chopped fresh basil
30ml/2 tbsp pine nuts, toasted
fresh basil sprig, to garnish

For the dressing
90ml/6 tbsp olive oil
30ml/2 tbsp wine vinegar
5ml/1 tsp balsamic vinegar (optional)
5ml/1 tsp wholegrain mustard
pinch of sugar
salt and ground black pepper

1 Cook the pasta in plenty of boiling salted water according to the instructions on the packet. Drain well and cool.

2 Using a sharp knife slice the tomatoes and mozzarella cheese into thin rounds.

3 Halve the avocado, remove the stone and peel off the skin. Slice the flesh lengthways.

4 Place all the dressing ingredients together in a small bowl and whisk until well blended.

5 Arrange the sliced tomato, mozzarella and avocado overlapping around the edge of a flat serving plate.

6 Toss the pasta with half the dressing and the chopped basil. Pile into the centre of the plate. Pour over the remaining dressing, scatter over the pine nuts and garnish with a sprig of fresh basil. Serve immediately.

Sesame Noodle Salad with Hot Peanuts

An Orient-inspired salad with crunchy vegetables and a light soy dressing. The hot peanuts make a surprisingly successful union with the cold noodles.

INGREDIENTS

Serves 4

350g/12oz Chinese egg noodles

2 carrots, peeled and cut into fine
　julienne strips

½ cucumber, peeled and cut into
　1cm/½in cubes

115g/4oz celeriac, peeled and cut into fine
　julienne strips

6 spring onions, finely sliced

8 canned water chestnuts, drained and
　finely sliced

175g/6oz beansprouts

1 small green chilli, seeded and
　finely chopped

30ml/2 tbsp sesame seeds, to serve

115g/4oz/1 cup peanuts, to serve

For the dressing

15ml/1 tbsp dark soy sauce

15ml/1 tbsp light soy sauce

15ml/1 tbsp clear honey

15ml/1 tbsp rice wine or dry sherry

15ml/1 tbsp sesame oil

1 Preheat the oven to 200°C/
400°F/Gas 6. Cook the egg
noodles in boiling water according
to the instructions on the packet.

2 Drain the noodles, refresh in
cold water, then drain again.

3 Mix the noodles with all of the
prepared vegetables.

4 Combine the dressing ingredients in a small bowl, then toss
into the noodle and vegetable
mixture. Divide the salad among
four serving plates.

5 Place the sesame seeds and
peanuts on separate baking
sheets and place in the oven. Take
the sesame seeds out of the
oven after 5 minutes and
continue to cook the peanuts for
a further 5 minutes until they are
evenly browned.

6 Sprinkle the sesame seeds and
peanuts evenly over each salad
portion and serve at once.

Seafood Spaghetti

This sauce offers a real, fresh seafood flavour. Serve with hunks of crusty French bread.

INGREDIENTS

Serves 4

350g/12oz spaghetti

50g/2oz/¼ cup butter

1 onion, chopped

1 red pepper, cored, seeded and
   coarsely chopped

2 garlic cloves, chopped

15ml/1 tbsp paprika

450g/1lb live mussels in the shell

150ml/¼ pint/⅔ cup dry white wine

30ml/2 tbsp chopped fresh parsley

225g/8oz/2 cups peeled prawns

150ml/¼ pint/⅔ cup crème fraîche

salt and ground black pepper

finely chopped fresh flat leaf parsley,
   to garnish

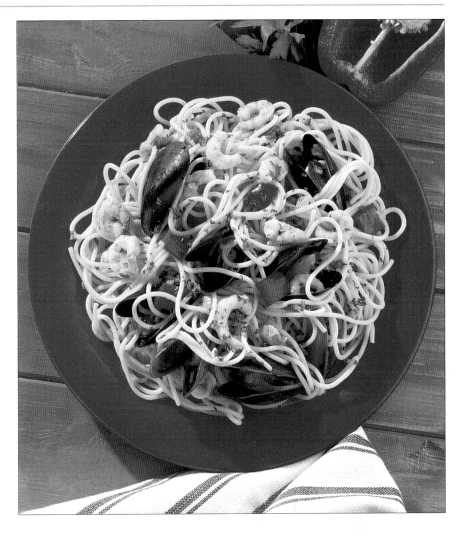

1 Cook the pasta in plenty of boiling salted water according to the instructions on the packet.

2 Melt the butter in a frying pan and fry the onion, pepper, garlic and paprika for 5 minutes until almost softened.

3 Rinse and scrub the mussels, making sure all the shells are tightly shut or they close when tapped sharply with the back of a knife. Discard any open shells.

4 Add the wine to the pan and bring to the boil.

5 Stir in the mussels, parsley and prawns, cover and simmer for about 5 minutes until the mussels have opened. Discard any mussels that remain closed.

6 Using a slotted spoon, remove the shellfish from the pan and keep warm. Bring the juices back to the boil and boil rapidly until reduced by half.

7 Stir in the crème fraîche until well blended. Season to taste. Return the shellfish to the pan and simmer for 1 minute to heat them throughly.

8 Drain the pasta thoroughly and divide it among four serving plates. Spoon over the shellfish and serve, garnished with the finely chopped fresh flat leaf parsley.

Minestrone with Pesto Toasts

This Italian mixed vegetable soup comes originally from Genoa, but the vegetables vary from region to region. This is also a great way to use up leftover vegetables.

INGREDIENTS

Serves 4

30ml/2 tbsp olive oil

2 garlic cloves, crushed

1 onion, halved and sliced

225g/8oz lean bacon, diced

2 small courgettes, quartered and sliced

50g/2oz French beans, chopped

2 small carrots, diced

2 celery sticks, finely chopped

1 bouquet garni

50g/2oz short cut macaroni

50g/2oz/½ cup frozen peas

200g/7oz can kidney beans, drained
   and rinsed

50g/2oz/1 cup shredded green cabbage

4 tomatoes, skinned and seeded

salt and ground black pepper

For the toasts

8 slices French bread

15ml/1 tbsp ready-made pesto sauce

15ml/1 tbsp grated Parmesan cheese

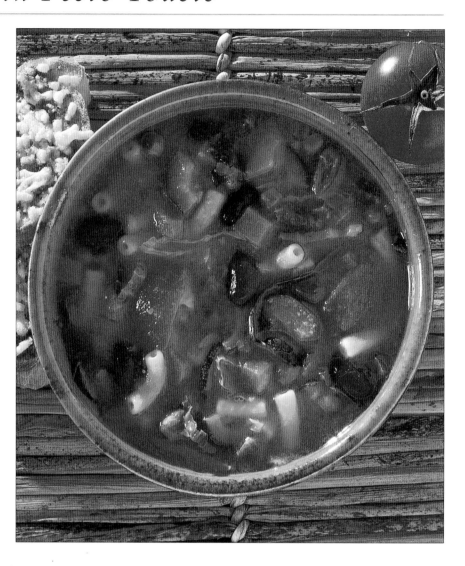

1 Heat the oil in a large pan and gently fry the garlic and onions for 5 minutes, until just softened. Add the bacon, courgettes, French beans, carrots and celery to the pan and stir-fry for 3 minutes.

COOK'S TIP

To appeal to children you could replace the macaroni with coloured pasta shapes such as shells, twists or bows if you like.

---

2 Pour 1.2 litres/2 pints/5 cups cold water over the vegetables and add the bouquet garni. Cover and simmer for 25 minutes.

3 Add the macaroni, peas and kidney beans and cook for 8 minutes.

4 Add the cabbage and tomatoes to the mixture and cook for a further 5 minutes.

5 Meanwhile, spread the bread slices with the pesto, sprinkle a little Parmesan over each one and brown lightly under a hot grill. Remove the bouquet garni, season and serve with the pesto toasts.

Butter Bean and Pesto Pasta

Buy good quality, ready-made pesto, rather than making your own, if you prefer. Pesto forms the basis of many very tasty sauces, and is especially good with butter beans.

INGREDIENTS

Serves 4

225g/8oz pasta shapes

freshly grated nutmeg

30ml/2 tbsp extra virgin olive oil

400g/14oz can butter beans, drained

45ml/3 tbsp pesto sauce

150ml/¼ pint/⅔ cup single cream

salt and ground black pepper

To serve

45ml/3 tbsp pine nuts

grated cheese (optional)

fresh basil sprigs, to garnish (optional)

1 Cook the pasta in plenty of boiling salted water until *al dente*, then drain, leaving it a little wet. Return the pasta to the pan, season, and stir in the nutmeg and extra virgin olive oil.

2 Heat the beans in a saucepan with the pesto and cream, stirring until the mixture begins to simmer. Toss the beans and pesto into the pasta and mix well.

3 Serve in bowls topped with pine nuts, and add a little grated cheese and some fresh basil sprigs if you wish.

Mediterranean Salad with Basil

A type of Salade Niçoise with pasta, conjuring up all the sunny flavours of the Mediterranean.

INGREDIENTS

Serves 4

225g/8oz chunky pasta shapes

175g/6oz fine green beans

2 large ripe tomatoes

50g/2oz fresh basil leaves

200g/7oz can tuna fish in oil, drained

2 hard-boiled eggs, shelled and sliced
    or quartered

50g/2oz can anchovy fillets, drained

capers and black olives

For the dressing

90ml/6 tbsp extra virgin olive oil

30ml/2 tbsp white wine vinegar or
    lemon juice

2 garlic cloves, crushed

2.5ml/½ tsp Dijon mustard

30ml/2 tbsp chopped fresh basil

salt and ground black pepper

1 Whisk all the ingredients for the dressing together and leave to infuse while you make the salad.

2 Cook the pasta in plenty of boiling salted water according to the instructions on the packet. Drain well and cool.

3 Trim the beans and blanch in boiling salted water for about 3 minutes. Drain and refresh in cold water.

4 Slice or quarter the tomatoes and arrange in the base of a bowl. Moisten with a little dressing and cover with a quarter of the basil leaves. Then cover with the beans. Moisten with a little more dressing and cover with a third of the remaining basil.

5 Cover with the pasta tossed in a little more dressing and half the remaining basil. Roughly flake the tuna, then add to the bowl.

6 Arrange the eggs on top, then finally scatter over the anchovy fillets, capers and black olives. Pour over the remaining dressing and garnish with the remaining basil. Serve immediately. Don't be tempted to chill this salad – all the flavour will be dulled.

Pasta, Melon and Prawn Salad

*Orange cantaloupe or Charentais
melon look spectacular in this salad.
Or try a mixture of ogen,
cantaloupe and water melon.*

INGREDIENTS

Serves 4–6

175g/6oz pasta shapes

225g/8oz/2 cups frozen prawns, thawed
   and drained

1 large or 2 small melons

60ml/4 tbsp olive oil

15ml/1 tbsp tarragon vinegar

30ml/2 tbsp snipped fresh chives or
   chopped parsley

herb sprigs, to garnish

shredded Chinese leaves, to serve

1 Cook the pasta in boiling salted
water according to the instructions on the packet. Drain well and
allow to cool.

2 Peel the prawns and discard
the shells.

3 Halve the melon and remove
the seeds with a teaspoon.
Carefully scoop the flesh into balls
with a melon baller and mix with
the prawns and pasta.

4 Whisk the oil, vinegar and
chopped herbs together. Pour
on to the prawn mixture and turn
to coat. Cover and chill for at least
30 minutes.

5 Meanwhile shred the Chinese
leaves and use to line a shallow
bowl or the empty melon halves.

6 Pile the prawn mixture on to
the Chinese leaves and garnish
with sprigs of herbs.

Chicken and Pasta Salad

This is a delicious way to use up leftover cooked chicken, and makes a filling meal.

Serves 4

225g/8oz tri-coloured pasta twists

30ml/2 tbsp ready-made pesto sauce

15ml/1 tbsp olive oil

1 beefsteak tomato

12 stoned black olives

225g/8oz cooked French beans, cut into 4cm/1½in lengths

350g/12oz cooked chicken, cubed

salt and ground black pepper

fresh basil, to garnish

3 Skin the tomato by placing it in boiling water for about 45 seconds and then into cold water, to loosen the skin.

4 Cut the tomato into small cubes and add to the pasta with the olives, seasoning and French beans. Add the cubed chicken. Toss gently together and transfer to a serving platter. Garnish with fresh basil.

1 Cook the pasta in plenty of boiling salted water according to the instructions on the packet.

2 Drain the pasta and rinse in plenty of cold running water. Put into a bowl and stir in the pesto sauce and olive oil.

MIDWEEK
MEALS

Aubergine Lasagne

This delicious lasagne is also suitable for home freezing.

Serves 4

3 aubergines, sliced

75ml/5 tbsp olive oil

2 large onions, finely chopped

2 × 400g/14oz cans chopped tomatoes

5ml/1 tsp dried mixed herbs

2–3 garlic cloves, crushed

6 sheets no-precook lasagne

salt and ground black pepper

For the cheese sauce

25g/1oz/2 tbsp butter

25g/1oz/2 tbsp plain flour

300ml/½ pint/1¼ cups milk

2.5ml/½ tsp English mustard

115g/4oz/8 tbsp grated mature Cheddar

15g/½oz/1 tbsp grated Parmesan cheese

1 Layer the sliced aubergine in a colander, sprinkling lightly with salt between each layer. Leave to stand for 1 hour, then rinse and pat dry with kitchen paper.

2 Heat 60ml/4 tbsp of the oil in a large pan, fry the aubergine and drain on kitchen paper. Add the remaining oil to the pan, cook the onions for 5 minutes, then stir in the tomatoes, herbs, garlic and seasoning. Bring to the boil and simmer, covered, for 30 minutes.

3 Melt the butter in a pan, stir in the flour and cook gently for 1 minute, stirring. Gradually stir in the milk. Bring to the boil, stirring, and cook for 2 minutes. Remove from the heat and stir in the mustard, cheeses and seasoning.

4 Preheat the oven to 200°C/ 400°F/Gas 6. Arrange half the aubergines in the base of an ovenproof dish, spoon over half the tomato sauce. Arrange three sheets of lasagne on top. Repeat.

5 Spoon over the cheese sauce, cover and bake for 30 minutes until lightly browned.

Macaroni Soufflé

This is generally a great favourite with children, and is rather like a light and fluffy macaroni cheese. Make sure you serve the soufflé immediately after it is cooked or it will sink dramatically.

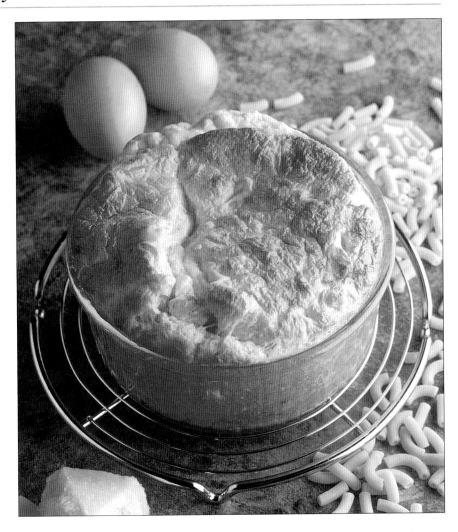

INGREDIENTS

Serves 3–4

75g/3oz short cut macaroni

melted butter, to coat

25g/1oz/3 tbsp dried breadcrumbs

50g/2oz/4 tbsp butter

5ml/1 tsp ground paprika

40g/1½oz/⅓ cup plain flour

300ml/½ pint/1¼ cups milk

75g/3oz Cheddar or Gruyère
   cheese, grated

50g/2oz Parmesan cheese, grated

3 eggs, separated

salt and ground black pepper

1 Cook the macaroni in plenty of boiling salted water according to the instructions on the packet. Drain well and set aside. Preheat the oven to 150°C/300°F/Gas 2.

2 Brush a 1.2 litre/2 pint/5 cup soufflé dish with melted butter, then coat evenly with the bread-crumbs, shaking out any excess from the pan.

3 Put the butter, paprika, flour and milk into a saucepan and slowly bring to the boil, whisking constantly until the mixture is smooth and thick.

4 Simmer the sauce for 1 minute, then remove from the heat and stir in the cheeses until melted. Season well and mix with the cooked macaroni.

5 Beat in the egg yolks. Whisk the egg whites until they form soft peaks and spoon a quarter into the sauce mixture to lighten it slightly.

6 Using a large metal spoon, carefully fold in the rest of the egg whites and transfer to the prepared soufflé dish.

7 Bake in the centre of the oven for about 40–45 minutes until the soufflé is risen and golden brown. The middle should wobble very slightly and the soufflé should be lightly creamy inside.

Greek Pasta Bake

Another excellent main meal (called pastitsio in Greece), this recipe is both economical and filling.

Serves 4

15ml/1 tbsp oil

450g/1lb/4 cups minced lamb

1 onion, chopped

2 garlic cloves, crushed

30ml/2 tbsp tomato purée

25g/1oz/2 tbsp plain flour

300ml/½ pint/1¼ cups lamb stock

2 large tomatoes

115g/4oz/1 cup pasta shapes

450g/1lb tub Greek yogurt

2 eggs

salt and ground black pepper

1 Preheat the oven to 190°C/ 375°F/Gas 5. Heat the oil in a large pan and fry the lamb for 5 minutes. Add the onion and garlic and continue to fry for a further 5 minutes.

2 Stir the tomato purée and flour into the pan. Cook for a further 1 minute.

3 Stir in the stock and season to taste. Bring to the boil and cook for 20 minutes.

4 Slice the tomatoes, place the meat in an ovenproof dish and arrange the tomatoes on top.

5 Cook the pasta shapes in boiling salted water for about 8–10 minutes or until *al dente*. Drain thoroughly.

6 Mix together the pasta, yogurt and eggs. Spoon on top of the tomatoes and then cook in the preheated oven for 1 hour. Serve with a crisp salad, if desired.

Bolognese Meat Sauce

This great meat sauce is a speciality of Bologna. It is delicious with tagliatelle or short pastas such as penne or conchiglie as well as spaghetti, and is indispensable in baked lasagne. It keeps well in the fridge for several days and can also be frozen for up to three months.

INGREDIENTS

Serves 6

25g/1oz/2 tbsp butter

60ml/4 tbsp olive oil

1 onion, finely chopped

25g/1oz/2 tbsp finely chopped pancetta or unsmoked bacon

1 carrot, finely sliced

1 celery stick, finely sliced

1 garlic clove, finely chopped

350g/12oz/3 cups lean minced beef

150ml/¼ pint/⅔ cup red wine

120ml/4fl oz/½ cup milk

400g/14oz can plum tomatoes, chopped, with their juice

1 bay leaf

1.5ml/¼ tsp fresh thyme leaves

salt and ground black pepper

cooked pasta, to serve

1 Heat the butter and oil in a heavy-based saucepan. Add the onion, and cook over a moderate heat for 3–4 minutes. Add the pancetta or bacon, and cook until the onion is translucent. Stir in the carrot, celery and garlic. Cook for a further 3–4 minutes.

2 Add the beef, and crumble it into the vegetables with a fork. Stir until the meat loses its red colour. Season to taste.

3 Pour in the wine, increase the heat slightly, and cook until the liquid evaporates, about 3–4 minutes. Add the milk and cook until it has evaporated.

4 Stir in the tomatoes with their juice, and the herbs. Bring the sauce to the boil. Reduce the heat to low and simmer, uncovered, for 1½–2 hours, stirring occasionally. Correct the seasoning before serving on a bed of pasta.

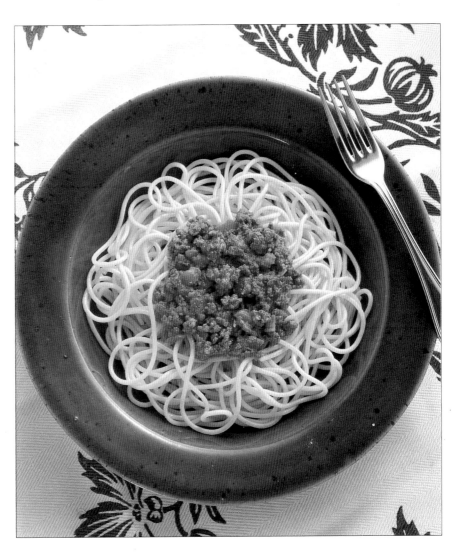

Pasta Carbonara

An Italian favourite, carbonara is traditionally served with spaghetti, but it is equally delicious made with fresh egg tagliatelle.

INGREDIENTS

Serves 4

350–450g/12oz–1lb fresh tagliatelle

15ml/1 tbsp olive oil

225g/8oz ham, bacon or pancetta, cut into 2.5cm/1in sticks

115g/4oz button mushrooms, sliced

4 eggs, lightly beaten

75ml/5 tbsp single cream

30ml/2 tbsp finely grated Parmesan cheese

salt and ground black pepper

fresh basil sprigs, to garnish

1 Cook the pasta in a pan of boiling salted water, with a little oil added, for 6–8 minutes or until *al dente*.

2 Meanwhile, heat the oil in a frying pan and add the meat. Fry for 3–4 minutes and then add the mushrooms and fry for a further 3–4 minutes. Turn off the heat and reserve. Lightly beat the eggs and cream together in a bowl and season well.

3 When the pasta is cooked, drain it well and return to the pan. Stir in the meat, mushrooms and any pan juices.

4 Pour in the eggs, cream and half the Parmesan cheese. Stir well and as you do this the eggs will cook in the heat of the pasta. Pile on to warmed serving plates, sprinkle with the remaining Parmesan and garnish with basil.

Pasta Bake

A popular British supper dish – replace the Cheddar with your family's favourite cheese.

INGREDIENTS

Serves 4

15ml/1 tbsp olive oil

275g/10oz macaroni

2 leeks, chopped

50g/2oz/4 tbsp butter

50g/2oz/½ cup plain flour

900ml/1½ pints/3¾ cups milk

225g/8oz/2 cups grated mature Cheddar cheese

30ml/2 tbsp fromage frais

5ml/1 tsp wholegrain mustard

50g/2oz/1 cup fresh breadcrumbs

25g/1oz/½ cup grated Double Gloucester cheese

salt and ground black pepper

15ml/1 tbsp chopped fresh parsley, to garnish

1 Preheat the oven to 180°C/ 350°F/Gas 4. Bring a large pan of salted water to the boil and add the olive oil. Then add the macaroni and leeks and boil gently for 10 minutes. Drain, rinse under cold water and reserve.

2 Heat the butter in a saucepan, stir in the flour and cook for about 1 minute. Remove from the heat and gradually add the milk, stirring well after each addition, until smooth. Return to the heat and stir continuously until the sauce is thickened.

3 Add the Cheddar cheese, fromage frais and mustard, mix well, and season with salt and ground black pepper.

4 Stir the drained macaroni and leeks into the cheese sauce and pile into a greased ovenproof dish. Level the top with the back of a spoon and sprinkle over the bread-crumbs and the grated Double Gloucester cheese.

5 Bake for 35–40 minutes. Serve hot, garnished with chopped fresh parsley.

Turkey Pastitsio

A traditional Greek pastitsio is made with minced beef, but this lighter version is just as tasty.

INGREDIENTS

Serves 4–6

450g/1lb/4 cups lean minced turkey

1 large onion, finely chopped

60ml/4 tbsp tomato purée

250ml/8fl oz/1 cup red wine or stock

5ml/1 tsp ground cinnamon

300g/11oz macaroni

300ml/½ pint/1¼ cups skimmed milk

25g/1oz/2 tbsp sunflower margarine

25g/1oz/3 tbsp plain flour

5ml/1 tsp grated nutmeg

2 tomatoes, sliced

60ml/4 tbsp wholemeal breadcrumbs

salt and ground black pepper

green salad, to serve

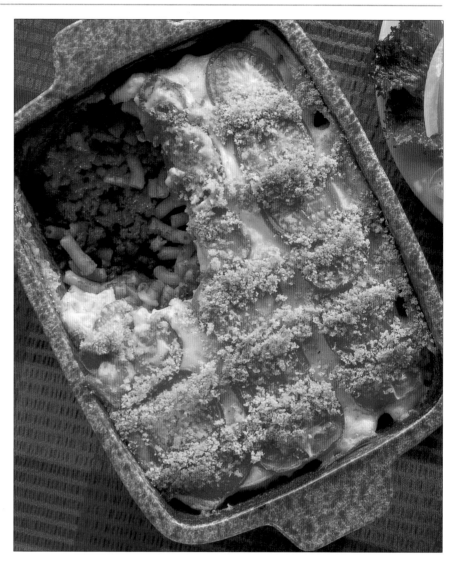

1 Preheat the oven to 220°C/ 425°F/Gas 7. Fry the turkey and onion in a non-stick pan without any fat, stirring until lightly browned.

2 Stir in the tomato purée, red wine or stock and cinnamon. Season, then cover and simmer for about 5 minutes.

3 Cook the macaroni in plenty of boiling salted water according to the instructions on the packet, until just tender, then drain.

4 Layer with the turkey mixture in a wide ovenproof dish.

5 Place the milk, margarine and flour in a saucepan and whisk over a moderate heat until thickened and smooth.

6 Whisk the nutmeg and seasoning to taste into the sauce, then pour evenly over the pasta. Arrange the tomato slices on top and sprinkle with lines of breadcrumbs.

7 Bake for 30–35 minutes, or until golden brown.

Fusilli with Turkey

Broccoli combines with the other ingredients to make a one-pan meal.

INGREDIENTS

Serves 4

675g/1½lb ripe, firm plum
    tomatoes, quartered
90ml/6 tbsp olive oil
5ml/1 tsp dried oregano
350g/12oz broccoli florets
1 small onion, sliced
5ml/1 tsp dried thyme
450g/1lb skinless, boneless turkey
    breast, cubed
3 garlic cloves, crushed
15ml/1 tbsp fresh lemon juice
450g/1lb fusilli
salt and ground black pepper

1 Preheat the oven to 200°C/
400°F/Gas 6. Place the plum
tomatoes in a baking dish. Add
15ml/1 tbsp of the oil, the oregano
and 2.5ml/½ tsp salt and stir.

2 Bake for 30–40 minutes, until
the tomatoes are just browned;
do not stir.

3 Meanwhile, bring a large
saucepan of salted water to the
boil. Add the broccoli florets and
cook until just tender, about
5 minutes. Drain and set aside.
(Alternatively, steam the broccoli
until tender.)

4 Heat 30ml/2 tbsp of the oil in a
large non-stick frying pan.

Add the onion, thyme, turkey and
2.5ml/½ tsp salt. Cook over a high
heat, stirring often, until the meat
is cooked and beginning to brown,
about 5–7 minutes. Add the garlic
and cook for a further 1 minute,
stirring frequently.

5 Remove from the heat. Stir in
the lemon juice and season
with ground black pepper. Set
aside and keep warm.

6 Cook the fusilli in plenty of
boiling salted water according
to the instructions on the packet
until *al dente*. Drain and place in a
large bowl. Toss the pasta with the
remaining oil.

7 Add the broccoli to the turkey
mixture, then stir into the
fusilli. Add the tomatoes and stir
gently to blend. Serve immediately.

Noodles with Italian Mushrooms

Porcini mushrooms give this sauce a wonderful depth.

Serves 2–4

25g/1oz dried Italian mushrooms (porcini)

175ml/6fl oz/¾ cup warm water

900g/2lb tomatoes, peeled, seeded and chopped or drained canned tomatoes

1.5ml/¼ tsp dried hot chilli flakes

45ml/3 tbsp olive oil

4 slices pancetta or rashers unsmoked back bacon, cut into thin strips

1 large garlic clove, finely chopped

350g/12oz tagliatelle or fettuccine

salt and ground black pepper

freshly grated Parmesan cheese, to serve

1 Put the mushrooms in a bowl and cover with the warm water. Leave to soak for 20 minutes.

2 Meanwhile, put the tomatoes in a saucepan with the chilli flakes and seasoning. If using canned tomatoes, crush them coarsely with a fork or potato masher. Bring to the boil, reduce the heat and simmer for about 30–40 minutes, until reduced to 750ml/1¼ pints/3 cups. Stir from time to time to prevent sticking.

3 When the mushrooms have finished soaking, lift them out and squeeze the remaining liquid over the bowl; set aside.

4 Carefully pour the soaking liquid into the tomatoes through a muslin-lined sieve. Simmer the tomatoes for a further 15 minutes.

5 Meanwhile, heat 30ml/2 tbsp of the oil in a frying pan. Add the strips of pancetta or bacon and fry until golden but not crisp. Add the garlic and mushrooms and fry for 3 minutes, stirring. Set aside.

6 Cook the pasta in plenty of boiling salted water until just *al dente*.

7 Add the bacon and mushroom mixture to the tomato sauce and mix well. Season with salt and ground black pepper.

8 Drain the pasta and return to the pan. Add the remaining oil and toss to coat the strands. Divide among hot plates, spoon the sauce on top and serve with freshly grated Parmesan cheese.

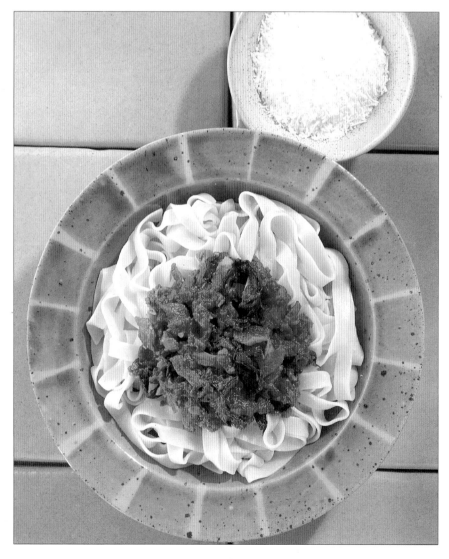

Chicken Lasagne

Based on the Italian beef lasagne, this is an excellent dish for entertaining guests of all ages. Serve simply with a green salad.

INGREDIENTS

Serves 8

30ml/2 tbsp olive oil

900g/2lb/8 cups minced raw chicken

225g/8oz rindless streaky bacon
    rashers, chopped

2 garlic cloves, crushed

450g/1lb leeks, sliced

225g/8oz carrots, diced

30ml/2 tbsp tomato purée

450ml/¾ pint/1¾ cups chicken stock

12 sheets (no-precook) green lasagne

For the cheese sauce

50g/2oz/4 tbsp butter

50g/2oz/4 tbsp plain flour

600ml/1 pint/2½ cups milk

115g/4oz/1 cup grated mature
    Cheddar cheese

1.5ml/¼ tsp English mustard powder

salt and ground black pepper

1 Heat the oil in a large flame-proof casserole and brown the minced chicken and bacon briskly, separating the pieces with a wooden spoon. Add the crushed garlic cloves, chopped leeks and diced carrots and cook for about 5 minutes until softened. Add the tomato purée, stock and seasoning. Bring to the boil, cover and simmer for 30 minutes.

2 For the sauce, melt the butter in a saucepan, add the flour and gradually blend in the milk, stirring until smooth. Bring to the boil, stirring all the time until thickened, and simmer for several minutes. Add half the grated Cheddar cheese and the mustard and season to taste.

3 Preheat the oven to 190°C/375°F/Gas 5. Layer the chicken mixture, lasagne and half the cheese sauce in a 2.5 litre/5 pint/12 cup ovenproof dish, starting and finishing with the chicken mixture.

4 Pour over the remaining cheese sauce, sprinkle over the remaining cheese and bake in the preheated oven for 1 hour, or until lightly browned.

Cannelloni Stuffed with Meat

Cannelloni are rectangles of home-made egg pasta which are spread with a filling, rolled up and baked in a sauce. In this recipe, they are baked in a béchamel sauce.

INGREDIENTS

Serves 6–8

30ml/2 tbsp olive oil

1 onion, very finely chopped

225g/8oz/1½ cups very lean minced beef

75g/3oz/½ cup finely chopped
   cooked ham

15ml/1 tbsp chopped fresh parsley

30ml/2 tbsp tomato purée, softened in
   15ml/1 tbsp warm water

1 egg

egg pasta sheets made with 2 eggs

750ml/1¼ pints/3 cups béchamel sauce

50g/2oz/½ cup freshly grated
   Parmesan cheese

40g/11/2oz/3 tbsp butter

salt and ground black pepper

1 Prepare the meat filling by heating the oil in a medium saucepan. Add the onion and sauté gently until translucent. Stir in the beef, crumbling it with a fork, and stirring constantly until it has lost its raw red colour. Cook for about 3–4 minutes.

2 Remove from the heat and turn the beef mixture into a bowl with the ham and parsley. Add the tomato purée mixture and the egg, and mix well. Season with salt and pepper. Set aside.

3 Make the egg pasta sheets. Do not let the pasta dry before cutting it into rectangles, about 13–15cm/5–6in long and as wide as they come from the machine (7.5cm/3in if you are not using a pasta machine).

4 Bring a very large pan of water to the boil. Place a large bowl of cold water near the cooker. Cover a large work surface with a tablecloth. Add salt to the rapidly boiling water. Drop in three or four of the egg pasta rectangles. Cook very briefly, for about 30 seconds. Plunge them into the cold water, shake off the excess and lay them out flat on the tablecloth. Continue until all the pasta has been cooked in this way.

5 Preheat the oven to 220°C/425°F/Gas 7. Select a shallow baking dish large enough to take all the cannelloni in one layer. Butter the dish and smear about 30–45ml/2–3 tbsp of béchamel sauce over the base.

6 Stir about one-third of the sauce into the meat filling. Spread a thin layer of filling on each pasta rectangle. Roll the rectangles up loosely starting from a long side, Swiss-roll style. Place the cannelloni in the baking dish with their open edges underneath.

7 Spoon the rest of the sauce over the cannelloni, pushing a little down between each pasta roll. Sprinkle the top with the grated Parmesan and dot with butter. Bake for about 20 minutes. Allow to rest for 5–8 minutes before serving on warmed plates.

Cheesy Pasta Bolognese

*Mozzarella gives the cheese sauce a
particularly creamy taste.*

INGREDIENTS

Serves 4

30ml/2 tbsp olive oil

1 onion, chopped

1 garlic clove, crushed

1 carrot, diced

2 celery sticks, chopped

2 rashers streaky bacon, finely chopped

5 button mushrooms, chopped

450g/1lb lean minced beef

120ml/4fl oz/½ cup red wine

15ml/1 tbsp tomato purée

200g/7oz can chopped tomatoes

fresh thyme sprig

225g/8oz dried penne

300ml/½ pint/1¼ cups milk

25g/1oz/2 tbsp butter

25g/1oz/2 tbsp flour

150g/5oz/1 cup cubed mozzarella cheese

60ml/4 tbsp grated Parmesan cheese

salt and ground black pepper

fresh basil sprigs, to garnish

1 Heat the oil in a pan and fry
the onion, garlic, carrot and
celery for 6 minutes, until the
onions have softened.

2 Add the bacon and continue
frying for 3–4 minutes. Stir in
the mushrooms, fry for 2 minutes,
then add the beef. Fry over a high
heat until well browned all over.

3 Pour in the red wine, the
tomato purée dissolved in
45ml/3 tbsp water, and the
tomatoes, then add the thyme and
season well. Bring to the boil, cover
the pan and simmer gently for
about 30 minutes.

4 Preheat the oven to 200°C/
400°F/Gas 6. Bring a pan of
water to the boil, add a little oil.
Cook the pasta for 10 minutes.

5 Meanwhile, place the milk,
butter and flour in a saucepan,
heat gently and whisk constantly
with a balloon whisk until the
mixture is thickened. Stir in
the cubed mozzarella cheese,
30ml/2 tbsp of the Parmesan
and season lightly.

6 Drain the pasta and stir into
the cheese sauce. Uncover the
tomato sauce and boil rapidly for
about 2 minutes to reduce.

7 Spoon the sauce into an
ovenproof dish, top with the
pasta mixture and sprinkle the
remaining 30ml/2 tbsp Parmesan
cheese evenly over the top. Bake
for 25 minutes until golden.
Garnish with basil and serve hot.

Thai Fried Noodles

An amazing array of tastes and textures make up this dish.

INGREDIENTS

Serves 4

225g/8oz thread egg noodles

60ml/4 tbsp vegetable oil

2 garlic cloves, finely chopped

175g/6oz pork tenderloin, sliced into thin strips

1 skinless boneless chicken breast, about 175g/6oz, sliced into thin strips

115g/4oz/1 cup cooked peeled shrimps (rinsed if canned)

45ml/3 tbsp lime or lemon juice

45ml/3 tbsp oriental fish sauce

30ml/2 tbsp soft light brown sugar

2 eggs, beaten

½ red chilli, seeded and finely chopped

50g/2oz/¼ cup beansprouts

60ml/4 tbsp roasted peanuts, chopped

3 spring onions, cut into 5cm/2in lengths and shredded

45ml/3 tbsp chopped fresh coriander

1 Place the noodles in a large pan of boiling water and leave to stand for about 5 minutes.

2 Meanwhile, heat 45ml/3 tbsp of the oil in a wok or large frying pan, add the garlic and cook for 30 seconds. Add the pork and chicken and stir-fry over a high heat until lightly browned, then add the shrimps and stir-fry for a further 2 minutes.

3 Add the lime or lemon juice, fish sauce and sugar, and stir-fry until the sugar has dissolved.

4 Drain the noodles and add to the pan with the remaining 15ml/1 tbsp oil. Toss all the ingredients together.

5 Pour in the beaten eggs. Stir-fry until almost set, then add the chilli and beansprouts. Divide the peanuts, spring onions and coriander leaves into two and add half to the pan. Stir-fry for

2 minutes, then tip the mixture on to a serving platter. Sprinkle on the remaining peanuts, spring onions and coriander and serve the noodles at once.

Rigatoni with Spicy Sausage

This is really a cheat's Bolognese sauce using the wonderful fresh spicy sausages sold in every good Italian delicatessen.

INGREDIENTS

Serves 4

450g/1lb fresh spicy Italian sausage

30ml/2 tbsp olive oil

1 onion, chopped

450ml/¾ pint/1¾ cups passata

150ml/¼ pint/⅔ cup dry red wine

6 sun-dried tomatoes in oil, drained

450g/1lb rigatoni or similar pasta

salt and ground black pepper

freshly grated Parmesan cheese, to serve

1 Squeeze the sausages out of their skins into a bowl and break up the meat.

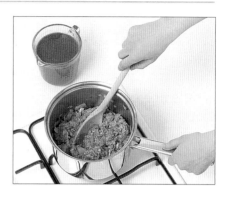

2 Heat the oil in a medium saucepan and add the onion. Cook for 5 minutes until soft and golden. Stir in the sausagemeat, browning it all over and breaking up the lumps with a wooden spoon. Pour in the passata and the wine. Bring to the boil.

3 Slice the sun-dried tomatoes and add to the sauce. Simmer for 3 minutes until reduced, stirring occasionally. Season.

4 Cook the pasta in plenty of boiling salted water according to the instructions on the packet. Drain well and top with the sauce. Serve with Parmesan cheese.

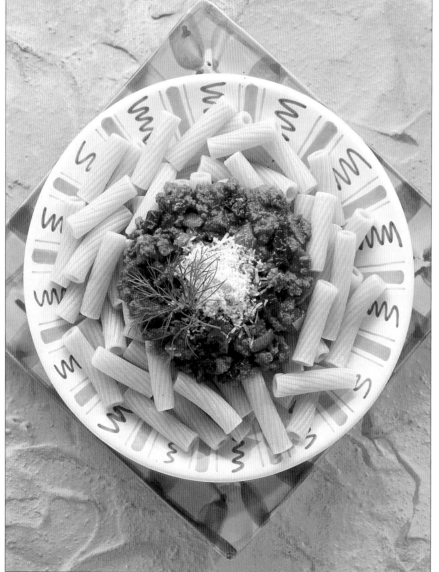

Pasta with Tomato and Smoky Bacon

A wonderful sauce to prepare in mid-summer when the tomatoes are ripe and sweet.

INGREDIENTS

Serves 4

900g/2lb ripe tomatoes

6 rashers smoked streaky bacon

50g/2oz/4 tbsp butter

1 onion, chopped

15ml/1 tbsp chopped fresh oregano or
   5ml/1 tsp dried

450g/1lb pasta, any variety

salt and ground black pepper

freshly grated Parmesan cheese, to serve

1 Plunge the tomatoes into boiling water for 1 minute, then into cold water. Slip off the skins. Halve the tomatoes, remove the seeds and cores and roughly chop the flesh.

2 Remove the rind from the streaky bacon and roughly chop the meat.

3 Melt the butter in a saucepan and add the bacon. Fry until lightly browned, then add the onion and cook gently for 5 minutes until softened. Add the tomatoes, salt, pepper and oregano. Simmer gently for 10 minutes.

4 Cook the pasta in plenty of boiling salted water according to the instructions on the packet. Drain well and toss with the sauce. Serve with plenty of freshly grated Parmesan cheese.

Rotolo di Pasta

A giant Swiss roll of pasta with a spinach filling, which is poached, sliced and baked with béchamel or tomato sauce. Use fresh homemade pasta for this recipe, or ask your local Italian deli to make a large sheet of pasta for you!

INGREDIENTS

Serves 6

700g/1½lb frozen chopped
    spinach, thawed
50g/2oz/4 tbsp butter
1 onion, chopped
100g/4oz ham or bacon, diced
225g/8oz ricotta or curd cheese
1 egg
freshly grated nutmeg
fresh spinach pasta made with 2 eggs and
    200g/7oz/1¾ cups flour
1.2 litres/2 pints/5 cups béchamel
    sauce, warmed
50g/2oz/½ cup freshly grated
    Parmesan cheese
salt and ground black pepper

1 Squeeze the excess moisture from the spinach and set aside.

2 Melt the butter in a saucepan and fry the onion until golden. Add the ham and fry until beginning to brown. Take off the heat and stir in the spinach. Cool slightly, then beat in the ricotta or curd cheese and the egg. Season with salt, pepper and nutmeg.

3 Roll the pasta out to a rectangle about 30 × 40cm/12 × 16in. Spread the filling all over, leaving a 1cm/½in border all round the edge of the rectangle.

4 Roll up from the shorter end and wrap in muslin to form a "sausage", tying the ends securely with string. Poach in a very large pan (or fish kettle) of simmering water for 20 minutes or until firm. Carefully remove, drain and then unwrap. Leave to cool.

5 When you are ready to finish the dish, preheat the oven to 200°C/400°F/Gas 6. Cut the pasta roll into 2.5cm/1in slices. Spoon a little béchamel sauce over the base of a shallow baking dish and arrange the slices on top, slightly overlapping each other.

6 Spoon over the remaining sauce, sprinkle with the cheese and bake for 15–20 minutes or until browned and bubbling. Allow to stand for a few minutes before serving.

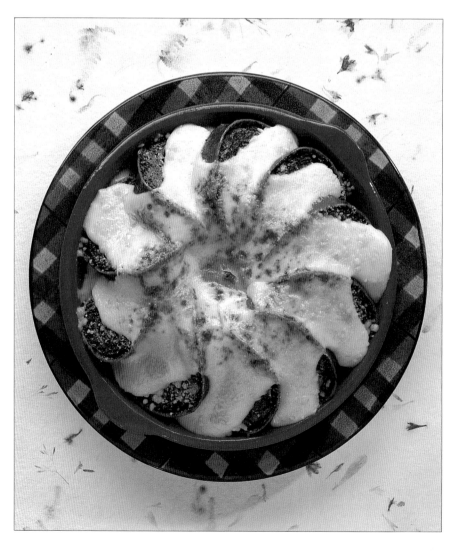

Pasta Timbales

An alternative way to serve pasta for a special occasion. Mixed with minced beef and tomato and baked in a lettuce parcel, it makes an impressive dish for a dinner party.

INGREDIENTS

Serves 4
8 cos lettuce leaves

For the filling
15ml/1 tbsp oil
175g/6oz/1½ cups minced beef
15ml/1 tbsp tomato purée
1 garlic clove, crushed
115g/4oz macaroni
salt and ground black pepper

For the sauce
25g/1oz/2 tbsp butter
25g/1oz/2 tbsp plain flour
250ml/8fl oz/1 cup double cream
30ml/2 tbsp chopped fresh basil

4 Line four 150ml/¼ pint/ ⅔ cup ramekin dishes with the cos lettuce leaves. Season the mince and spoon into the lettuce-lined ramekins.

5 Fold the lettuce leaves over the filling and place in a roasting tin half-filled with boiling water. Cover and cook for 20 minutes.

6 For the sauce melt the butter in a pan. Add the flour and cook for 1 minute. Stir in the cream and fresh basil. Season and bring to the boil, stirring all the time. Turn out the timbales and serve with the creamy basil sauce, and a crisp green salad if liked.

1 Preheat the oven to 180°C/ 350°F/Gas 4. For the filling, heat the oil in a large pan and fry the minced beef for 7 minutes. Add the tomato purée and garlic and cook for 5 minutes.

2 Cook the macaroni in boiling salted water for 8–10 minutes or until *al dente*. Drain.

3 Mix together the pasta and minced beef mixture.

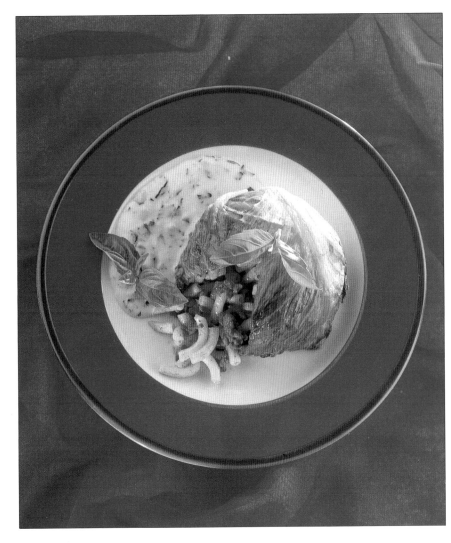

Spaghetti alla Carbonara

It has been said that this dish was originally cooked by Italian coal miners or charcoal-burners, hence the name "carbonara". The secret of its creamy sauce is not to overcook the egg.

INGREDIENTS

Serves 4

175g/6oz unsmoked streaky bacon

1 garlic clove, chopped

3 eggs

450g/1lb spaghetti

60ml/4 tbsp freshly grated
  Parmesan cheese

salt and ground black pepper

1 Dice the bacon and place in a medium saucepan. Fry in its own fat with the garlic until brown. Keep warm until needed.

2 Whisk the eggs together in a mixing bowl.

3 Cook the spaghetti in plenty of boiling salted water according to the instructions on the packet or until *al dente*. Drain well.

4 Quickly turn the spaghetti into the pan with the bacon and stir in the eggs, a little salt, lots of pepper and half the cheese. Toss well to mix. The eggs should half-cook in the heat from the pasta. Serve in warmed bowls with the remaining Parmesan cheese sprinkled over each portion.

Pasta with Bolognese Sauce

Traditional Bolognese sauce contains chicken livers to add richness, but you can leave them out and replace with an equal quantity of minced beef.

INGREDIENTS

Serves 4–6

75g/3oz pancetta or bacon

115g/4oz chicken livers

50g/2oz/4 tbsp butter, plus extra for
   tossing the pasta

1 onion, finely chopped

1 carrot, diced

1 celery stick, finely chopped

225g/8oz/2 cups lean minced beef

30ml/2 tbsp tomato purée

120ml/4fl oz/½ cup white wine

200ml/7fl oz/scant 1 cup beef stock
   or water

freshly grated nutmeg

450g/1lb tagliatelle, spaghetti or fettuccine

salt and ground black pepper

freshly grated Parmesan cheese, to serve

1 Dice the pancetta or bacon. Trim the chicken livers, removing any fat or gristle and any "green" bits which will be bitter if left on. Roughly chop the livers.

2 Melt 50g/2oz/4 tbsp butter in a saucepan and add the bacon. Cook for 2-3 minutes until just beginning to brown. Then add the onion, carrot and celery and brown these too.

3 Stir in the beef and brown over a high heat, breaking it up with a spoon. Add the chicken livers and cook for 2-3 minutes. Add the tomato purée with the wine and stock or water. Season well with salt, pepper and nutmeg. Bring to the boil, cover and simmer for 35 minutes.

4 Cook the pasta in plenty of boiling salted water according to the instructions on the packet or until *al dente*. Drain well and toss with the extra butter. Toss the meat sauce with the pasta and serve with plenty of grated Parmesan cheese.

Home-made Ravioli

It is a pleasure to make your own fresh pasta and you might be surprised at just how easy it is to fill and shape ravioli. Allow a little more time than you would for ready-made or dried pasta. A blender or food processor will save you time and effort in making and kneading the dough. A pasta-making machine helps with the rolling out, but both these jobs can be done by hand if necessary.

Serves 6

200g/7oz/1¾ cups strong plain flour
5ml/½ tsp salt
15ml/1 tbsp olive oil
2 eggs, beaten

For the filling

1 small red onion, finely chopped
1 small green pepper, finely chopped
1 carrot, coarsely grated
15ml/1 tbsp olive oil
50g/2oz/½ cup walnuts, chopped
115g/4oz/½ cup ricotta cheese
30ml/2 tbsp freshly grated Parmesan or
    pecorino cheese
15ml/1 tbsp chopped fresh marjoram
    or basil
salt and ground black pepper
extra oil or melted butter, to serve

1 Sift the flour and salt into a blender or food processor. With the machine running, trickle in the oil and eggs and blend to a stiff but smooth dough.

2 Allow the machine to run for at least 1 minute if possible, otherwise remove the dough and knead by hand for 5 minutes.

3 If you are using a pasta machine, break off small balls of dough and feed them through the rollers, several times, according to the instructions that come with the machine.

4 If rolling the pasta by hand, divide the dough into two and roll out on a lightly floured surface to a thickness of about 5mm/¼in.

5 Fold the pasta into three and re-roll. Repeat this up to six times until the dough is smooth and no longer sticky. Roll the pasta slightly more thinly each time.

6 Keep the rolled dough under clean, dry dish towels while you complete the rest and make the filling. You should aim to have an even number of pasta sheets, all the same size.

7 Fry the onion, pepper and carrot in the oil for 5 minutes, then allow to cool. Mix with the walnuts, cheeses, herbs and lots of seasoning.

8 Lay out a pasta sheet and place small scoops of the filling in neat rows about 5cm/2in apart.

Brush between the mounds of filling with a little water and then place another pasta sheet on the top to cover.

9 Press down well in between the rows then, using a ravioli or pastry cutter, cut into squares. If the edges pop open, press them back gently with your fingers.

10 Leave the ravioli to dry in the fridge, then boil in plenty of lightly salted water for just 5 minutes.

11 Toss the cooked ravioli in a little oil or melted butter before serving with homemade tomato sauce or extra cheese.

Autumn Glory

Glorious pumpkin shells summon up the delights of autumn and seem too good simply to throw away. Use one instead as a serving dish. Pumpkin and pasta make marvellous partners, especially as a main course served from the baked shell.

INGREDIENTS

Serves 4

1.75kg/4–4½lb pumpkin
1 onion, sliced
2.5cm/1in piece fresh root ginger
45ml/3 tbsp extra virgin olive oil
1 courgette, sliced
115g/4oz sliced mushrooms
400g/14oz can chopped tomatoes
75g/3oz pasta shells
450ml/¾ pint/1¾ cups stock
60ml/4 tbsp fromage frais
30ml/2 tbsp chopped fresh basil
salt and ground black pepper

1 Preheat the oven to 180°C/350°F/Gas 4. Cut the top off the pumpkin with a large, sharp knife and scoop out and discard the pumpkin seeds.

2 Using a small sharp knife and a sturdy tablespoon, cut and scrape out as much flesh from the pumpkin shell as possible, then chop the flesh into rough chunks.

3 Bake the pumpkin with its lid on for 45 minutes–1 hour until the inside begins to soften.

4 Meanwhile, make the filling. Gently fry the onion, ginger and pumpkin flesh in the olive oil for about 10 minutes, stirring the mixture occasionally.

5 Add the sliced courgette and mushrooms and cook for a further 3 minutes, then stir in the tomatoes, pasta shells and stock. Season well, bring to the boil, then cover the pan and simmer gently for about 10 minutes.

6 Stir the fromage frais and basil into the pasta and spoon the mixture into the pumpkin. It may not be possible to fit all the filling into the pumpkin shell, so serve the rest separately if necessary.

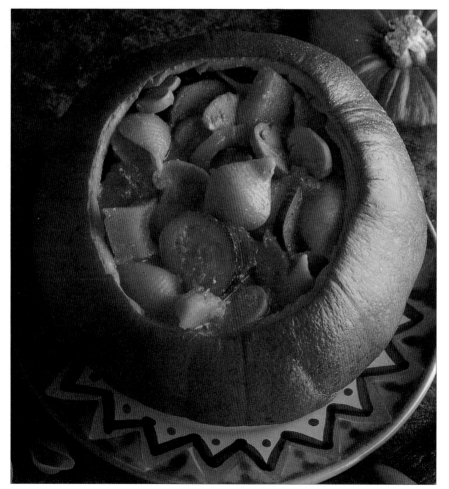

Pasta with Caponata

The Sicilians have an excellent sweet-and-sour vegetable dish, called caponata, *which goes wonderfully well with pasta.*

INGREDIENTS

Serves 4

1 aubergine, cut into sticks

2 courgettes, cut into sticks

8 baby onions, peeled or 1 large
   onion, sliced

2 garlic cloves, crushed

1 large red pepper, sliced

60ml/4 tbsp olive oil, preferably
   extra virgin

450ml/¾ pint/1¾ cups tomato juice

150ml/¼ pint/⅔ cup water

30ml/2 tbsp balsamic vinegar

juice of 1 lemon

15ml/1 tbsp sugar

30ml/2 tbsp sliced black olives

30ml/2 tbsp capers

400g/14oz tagliatelle or other
   ribbon pasta

salt and ground black pepper

1 Lightly salt the aubergine and courgettes and leave them to drain in a colander for 30 minutes. Rinse and pat dry thoroughly with kitchen paper.

2 In a large saucepan, lightly fry the onions, garlic and pepper in the oil for 5 minutes, then stir in the aubergine and courgettes and fry for a further 5 minutes.

3 Stir in the tomato juice and the water. Stir well, bring the mixture to the boil, then add all the rest of the ingredients except the pasta. Season to taste and simmer for 10 minutes.

4 Meanwhile, cook the pasta according to the instructions on the packet, then drain. Serve the *caponata* with the pasta.

Broccoli and Ricotta Cannelloni

*This dish will be enjoyed by both
vegetarians and meat-eaters.*

INGREDIENTS

Serves 4

12 dried cannelloni tubes, 7.5cm/3in long

450g/1lb/4 cups broccoli florets

75g/3oz/1½ cups fresh breadcrumbs

150ml/¼ pint/⅔ cup milk

60ml/4 tbsp olive oil, plus extra
    for brushing

225g/8oz/1 cup ricotta cheese

pinch of grated nutmeg

90ml/6 tbsp grated Parmesan or
    pecorino cheese

salt and ground black pepper

30ml/2 tbsp pine nuts, for sprinkling

For the tomato sauce

30ml/2 tbsp olive oil

1 onion, finely chopped

1 garlic clove, crushed

2 x 400g/14oz cans chopped tomatoes

15ml/1 tbsp tomato purée

4 black olives, stoned and chopped

5ml/1 tsp dried thyme

1 Preheat the oven to 190°C/
375°F/Gas 5 and lightly grease
an ovenproof dish with olive oil.
Bring a large saucepan of water to
the boil, add a little olive oil and
simmer the cannelloni tubes,
uncovered, for about 6–7 minutes,
or until nearly cooked.

2 Meanwhile, steam or boil the
broccoli for 10 minutes, until
tender. Drain the pasta, rinse
under cold water and reserve.
Drain the broccoli and leave to
cool, then place in a blender or
food processor and process until
smooth. Set aside.

3 Place the breadcrumbs in a
bowl, add the milk and oil and
stir until softened. Add the ricotta,
broccoli purée, nutmeg, 60ml/

4 tbsp of the Parmesan cheese and
seasoning, then set aside.

4 To make the sauce, heat the oil
in a frying pan; add the onion
and garlic. Fry for 5–6 minutes,
until softened, then stir in the
tomatoes, tomato purée, black
olives, thyme and seasoning. Boil
rapidly for 2–3 minutes, then pour
into the base of the dish.

5 Spoon the cheese mixture into
a piping bag fitted with a
1cm/½in nozzle. Carefully open
the cannelloni tubes. Standing
each one upright on a board, pipe
the filling into each tube. Lay them
in rows in the tomato sauce.

6 Brush the tops of the cannelloni with a little olive oil and
sprinkle over the remaining
Parmesan cheese and pine nuts.
Bake for about 25–30 minutes,
until golden on top.

Baked Tortellini with Three Cheeses

Serve this straight out of the oven while the cheese is still runny. If smoked mozzarella cheese is not available, try using a smoked German cheese or even grated smoked Cheddar.

INGREDIENTS

Serves 4–6

450g/1lb fresh tortellini

2 eggs

350g/12oz/1½ cups ricotta or curd cheese

25g/1oz/2 tbsp butter

25g/1oz fresh basil leaves

115g/4oz smoked mozzarella cheese

60ml/4 tbsp freshly grated
   Parmesan cheese

salt and ground black pepper

1 Preheat the oven to 190°C/ 375°F/Gas 5. Cook the fresh tortellini in plenty of boiling salted water according to the instructions on the packet. Drain well.

2 Beat the eggs with the ricotta or curd cheese and season well with salt and pepper. Use the butter to grease an ovenproof dish. Spoon in half the tortellini, pour over half the cheese mixture and cover with half the basil leaves.

3 Cover with the mozzarella and remaining basil. Top with the rest of the tortellini and spread over the remaining ricotta or curd cheese mixture.

4 Sprinkle evenly with the Parmesan cheese. Bake in the oven for 35–45 minutes or until golden brown and bubbling.

Cannelloni

This version of a classic Italian dish introduces a variety of vegetables which are topped with a traditional cheese sauce.

INGREDIENTS

Serves 4

8 cannelloni tubes
115g/4oz spinach

For the filling
15ml/1 tbsp oil
175g/6oz/1½ cups minced beef
2 garlic cloves, crushed
25g/1oz/2 tbsp plain flour
120ml/4fl oz/½ cup beef stock
1 small carrot, finely chopped
1 small yellow courgette, chopped
salt and ground black pepper

For the sauce
25g/1oz/2 tbsp butter
25g/1oz/2 tbsp plain flour
250ml/8fl oz/1 cup milk
50g/2oz/½ cup freshly grated
   Parmesan cheese

1 Preheat the oven to 180°C/ 350°F/Gas 4. For the filling, heat the oil in a large pan. Add the minced beef and garlic. Cook for 5 minutes.

2 Add the flour and cook for a further 1 minute. Slowly stir in the stock and bring to the boil.

3 Add the carrot and courgette. Season. Cook for 10 minutes.

4 Spoon the mince mixture into the cannelloni tubes and place in an ovenproof dish.

5 Blanch the spinach in boiling water for 3 minutes. Drain well and place on top of the cannelloni tubes in the dish.

6 For the sauce melt the butter in a pan. Add the flour and cook for 1 minute. Pour in the milk, add the grated cheese and season well. Bring to the boil, stirring all the time. Pour over the cannelloni and spinach and bake for 30 minutes. Serve with tomatoes and a crisp green salad, if liked.

Pasta Spirals with Lentils and Cheese

This surprising combination works
extremely well.

INGREDIENTS

Serves 4

15ml/1 tbsp olive oil

1 onion, chopped

1 garlic clove, chopped

1 carrot, cut into matchsticks

350g/12oz pasta spirals, such as fusilli

65g/2½oz/½ cup green lentils, boiled for
   25 minutes

15ml/1 tbsp tomato purée

15ml/1 tbsp chopped fresh oregano

150ml/¼ pint/⅔ cup vegetable stock

225g/8oz/2 cups grated Cheddar cheese

salt and ground black pepper

freshly grated cheese, to serve

1 Heat the oil in a large frying
pan and fry the onion and
garlic for 3 minutes. Add the carrot
and cook for a further 5 minutes.

COOK'S TIP

Tomato purée is sold in small
cans and tubes. If you use a can
for this small amount, you can
keep the remainder fresh by
transferring it to a bowl,
covering it with a thin layer of
olive oil and putting it in the
fridge until needed.

2 Cook the pasta in plenty of
boiling salted water according
to the instructions on the packet.

3 Add the lentils, tomato purée
and oregano to the frying pan,
stir, cover and cook for 3 minutes.

4 Add the stock and salt and
pepper to the pan. Cover and
simmer for 10 minutes. Add the
grated Cheddar cheese.

5 Drain the pasta thoroughly and
stir into the sauce to coat. Serve
with plenty of extra grated cheese.

Pasta Spirals with Chicken and Tomato

A recipe for a speedy supper – serve this dish with a mixed bean salad.

INGREDIENTS

Serves 4

15ml/1 tbsp olive oil

1 onion, chopped

1 carrot, chopped

50g/2oz sun-dried tomatoes in olive oil, drained weight

1 garlic clove, chopped

400g/14oz can chopped tomatoes, drained

15ml/1 tbsp tomato purée

150ml/¼ pint/⅔ cup chicken stock

350g/12oz fusilli

225g/8oz chicken, diagonally sliced

salt and ground black pepper

fresh mint sprigs, to garnish

3 Stir the garlic, tomatoes, tomato purée and stock into the onions and carrots and bring to the boil. Simmer for 10 minutes, stirring occasionally.

4 Cook the pasta in plenty of boiling salted water according to the instructions on the packet.

5 Pour the sauce into a blender or food processor and process until smooth.

6 Return the sauce to the pan and stir in the sun-dried tomatoes and chicken. Bring back to the boil and then simmer for 10 minutes until the chicken is cooked. Adjust the seasoning, if necessary.

7 Drain the pasta thoroughly and toss in the sauce. Serve at once, garnished with sprigs of fresh mint.

1 Heat the oil in a large frying pan and fry the onion and carrot for 5 minutes, stirring the vegetables occasionally.

2 Chop the sun-dried tomatoes and set aside until needed.

Lasagne al Forno

The classic version of this dish is pasta layered with meat sauce and creamy béchamel sauce. You could vary it by using mozzarella cheese instead of the béchamel sauce, or by mixing ricotta cheese, Parmesan and herbs together instead of the traditional meat sauce.

INGREDIENTS

Serves 4–6

about 12 sheets dried lasagne

1 quantity Bolognese Sauce

about 50g/2oz/½ cup freshly grated
   Parmesan cheese

tomato slices and parsley sprig, to garnish

For the béchamel sauce

900ml/1½ pints/3¾ cups milk

sliced onion, carrot and celery

a few whole black peppercorns

50g/2oz/½ cup butter

75g/3oz/¾ cup plain flour

freshly grated nutmeg

salt and ground black pepper

1 First make the béchamel sauce. Pour the milk into a saucepan and add the vegetables and peppercorns. Bring to boiling point, remove from the heat and leave to infuse for at least 30 minutes.

2 Strain the milk into a jug. Then melt the butter in the same saucepan and stir in the flour. Cook, stirring, for 2 minutes.

3 Remove from the heat and add the milk all at once, whisk well and return to the heat. Bring to the boil, whisking all the time, then simmer for 2–3 minutes, stirring constantly until thickened. Season to taste with nutmeg, salt and ground black pepper.

4 Preheat the oven to 180°C/ 350°F/Gas 4. If necessary, cook the sheets of lasagne in plenty of boiling salted water according to the instructions on the packet. Lift out with a slotted spoon and drain on a clean dish towel. Spoon a third of the meat sauce into a buttered baking-dish.

5 Place four sheets of lasagne over the meat sauce. Spread with one-third of the béchamel sauce. Repeat twice more, finishing with a layer of béchamel sauce covering the whole top.

6 Sprinkle with Parmesan cheese and bake in the oven for about 45 minutes until brown. Serve garnished with tomato slices and a sprig of parsley.

Baked Lasagne with Meat Sauce

This lasagne made from egg pasta with homemade meat and béchamel sauce is exquisite.

INGREDIENTS

Serves 8–10

2 quantities Bolognese Meat Sauce

egg pasta sheets made with 3 eggs or
   400g/14oz dried lasagne

115g/4oz/1 cup grated Parmesan cheese

40g/1½oz/3 tbsp butter

For the béchamel sauce

750ml/1¼ pints/3 cups milk

1 bay leaf

3 mace blades

115g/4oz/½ cup butter

75g/3oz/¾ cup plain flour

salt and ground black pepper

1 Prepare the meat sauce and set aside. Butter a large shallow baking dish, preferably rectangular or square.

COOK'S TIP

If you are using dried or bought pasta, follow step 4, but boil the lasagne in just two batches, and stop the cooking about 4 minutes before the recommended cooking time on the packet has elapsed. Rinse in cold water and lay the pasta out the same way as for the egg pasta.

---

2 Make the béchamel sauce by gently heating the milk with the bay leaf and mace in a small saucepan. Melt the butter in a medium heavy-based saucepan. Add the flour, and mix well with a wire whisk. Cook for 2–3 minutes. Strain the hot milk into the flour and butter, and mix smoothly with the whisk. Bring the sauce to the boil, stirring constantly, and cook for a further 4–5 minutes. Season with salt and pepper and set aside.

3 Make the pasta. Do not let it dry out before cutting it into rectangles measuring about 11cm/4½in wide and the same length as the baking dish (this will make it easier to assemble later). Preheat the oven to 200°C/400°F/Gas 6.

4 Bring a very large pan of water to the boil. Place a large bowl of cold water near the cooker. Cover a large work surface with a tablecloth. Add salt to the rapidly boiling water. Drop in 3 or 4 of the egg pasta rectangles. Cook very briefly, about 30 seconds. Remove from the pan, using a slotted spoon, and drop into the cold water for about 30 seconds. Pull them out of the water, shaking off the excess water. Lay them out flat without overlapping on the table-cloth. Continue with all the remaining pasta and trimmings.

5 To assemble the lasagne, spread one large spoonful of the meat sauce over the base of the dish. Arrange a layer of pasta in the dish, cutting it with a sharp knife so that it fits well.

6 Cover with a thin layer of meat sauce, then one of béchamel. Sprinkle with a little cheese. Repeat the layers in the same order, and ending with a layer of pasta coated with béchamel. Do not make more than about 6 layers of pasta. Use the pasta trimmings to patch any gaps in the pasta. Sprinkle the top with grated Parmesan cheese, and dot with butter.

7 Bake in the preheated oven for 20 minutes, or until brown on top. Remove from the oven and allow to stand for about 5 minutes before serving. Serve directly from the baking dish, cutting out rectangular or square sections for each helping.

Leek and Chèvre Lasagne

An unusual and lighter than average lasagne using a soft French goat's cheese. The pasta sheets are not so chewy if boiled briefly first, or you could use no-precook lasagne instead if you prefer.

INGREDIENTS

Serves 6

6–8 lasagne sheets

1 large aubergine, sliced

3 leeks, thinly sliced

30ml/2 tbsp olive oil

2 red peppers, roasted

200g/7oz chèvre, broken into pieces

50g/2oz/½ cup freshly grated pecorino or
   Parmesan cheese

For the sauce

65g/2½oz/9 tbsp plain flour

65g/2½oz/5 tbsp butter

900ml/1½ pints/3¾ cups milk

2.5ml/½ tsp ground bay leaves

freshly grated nutmeg

salt and ground black pepper

1 Blanch the pasta sheets in plenty of boiling water for just 2 minutes. Drain and place on a clean dish towel.

2 Lightly salt the aubergine slices and place in a colander to drain for 30 minutes, then rinse and pat dry with kitchen paper.

3 Preheat the oven to 190°C/ 375°F/Gas 5. Lightly fry the leeks in the oil for 5 minutes, until softened. Peel the roasted peppers and cut into strips.

4 To make the sauce, put the flour, butter and milk into a saucepan and bring to the boil, stirring constantly until thickened. Add the ground bay leaves, nutmeg and seasoning. Simmer the sauce for a further 2 minutes.

5 In a greased shallow casserole, layer the leeks, lasagne sheets, aubergine, chèvre and pecorino or Parmesan. Trickle the sauce over the layers, ensuring that plenty goes in-between.

6 Finish with a layer of sauce and grated cheese. Bake in the oven for 30 minutes, or until bubbling and browned on top. Serve immediately.

Macaroni and Blue Cheese

*The blue cheese gives this simple
dish a new twist.*

INGREDIENTS

Serves 6

450g/1lb macaroni

900ml/1½ pints/3¾ cups milk

50g/2oz/4 tbsp butter

75g/3oz/6 tbsp plain flour

1.5ml/¼ tsp salt

225g/8oz blue cheese, crumbled

ground black pepper

1 Preheat the oven to 180°C/
350°F/Gas 4. Lightly grease a
33 × 23cm/12 × 9in baking dish.

2 Cook the macaroni in plenty of
boiling salted water according
to the instructions on the packet,
or until *al dente*. Drain and rinse
under cold water. Place in a large
bowl and set aside.

3 In another pan, bring the milk
to the boil and set aside.

4 Melt the butter in a heavy-
based saucepan over a low
heat. Whisk in the flour and cook
for 5 minutes, whisking continuously. Be careful not to let the
mixture brown.

5 Remove from the heat and
whisk the hot milk into the
butter and flour mixture. When
smoothly blended, return to a
medium heat and continue
cooking for about 5 minutes,
whisking constantly until the sauce
is thick. Add the salt.

6 Add the sauce to the macaroni.
Add three-quarters of the
crumbled blue cheese and stir well.
Transfer the macaroni mixture to
the prepared baking dish and
spread in an even layer.

7 Sprinkle the remaining cheese
evenly over the surface. Bake
for 25 minutes, until bubbling hot.

8 If desired, lightly brown the
top of the macaroni and cheese
under the grill for 3–4 minutes.
Serve hot, sprinkled with ground
black pepper to taste.

QUICK
& EASY

Linguine with Pesto Sauce

Pesto originates in Liguria, where the sea breezes are said to give the local basil a particularly fine flavour. It is traditionally made with a pestle and mortar, but it is easier to make in a food processor or blender. Freeze any spare pesto in an ice-cube tray for later use.

INGREDIENTS

Serves 5–6

65g/2½oz/¾ cup fresh basil leaves

3–4 cloves garlic, peeled

45ml/3 tbsp pine nuts

2.5ml/½ tsp salt

75ml/5 tbsp olive oil

50g/2oz/½ cup freshly grated
   Parmesan cheese

60ml/4 tbsp freshly grated
   pecorino cheese

ground black pepper

500g/1¼lb linguine

1 Place the basil, garlic, pine nuts, salt and olive oil in a blender or food processor and process until smooth. Remove to a bowl. If desired, the sauce may be frozen at this point, before the cheeses are added.

2 Stir in the cheeses (use all Parmesan if pecorino is not available). Taste for seasoning.

3 Cook the pasta in a large pan of rapidly boiling salted water until it is *al dente*. Just before draining, take about 60ml/4 tbsp of the cooking water and stir into the pesto sauce.

4 Drain the pasta thoroughly and toss it together with the sauce. Serve immediately.

Pappardelle with Beans and Mushrooms

A mixture of wild and cultivated mushrooms help to give this dish a rich and nutty flavour.

INGREDIENTS

Serves 4

30ml/2 tbsp olive oil

50g/2oz/4 tbsp butter

2 shallots, chopped

2–3 garlic cloves, crushed

675g/1½lb mixed mushrooms, thickly sliced

4 sun-dried tomatoes in oil, drained and chopped

90ml/6 tbsp dry white wine

400g/14oz can borlotti beans, drained

45ml/3 tbsp grated Parmesan cheese

30ml/2 tbsp chopped fresh parsley

salt and ground black pepper

cooked pappardelle, to serve

1 Heat the oil and butter in a frying pan and fry the shallots until they are soft.

2 Add the garlic and mushrooms and fry for 3–4 minutes. Stir in the sun-dried tomatoes, wine and add seasoning to taste.

3 Stir in the borlotti beans and cook for 5–6 minutes, until most of the liquid has evaporated from the pan and the beans are warmed through.

4 Stir in the grated Parmesan cheese. Sprinkle with parsley and serve immediately with freshly cooked pappardelle.

Orecchiette with Broccoli

Puglia, in southern Italy, specializes in imaginative pasta and vegetable combinations. Using the broccoli cooking water for boiling the pasta gives it more of the vegetable's lovely fresh flavour.

INGREDIENTS

Serves 6

800g/1¾lb broccoli

450g/1lb orecchiette or penne

90ml/6 tbsp olive oil

3 garlic cloves, finely chopped

6 anchovy fillets in oil

salt and ground black pepper

1 Peel the stems of the broccoli, starting from the base and pulling up towards the florets with a knife. Discard the woody parts of the stem. Cut the florets and stems into 5cm/2in pieces.

2 Bring a large pan of water to the boil. Drop in the broccoli and boil until barely tender, about 5–8 minutes. Remove the broccoli pieces from the pan to a serving bowl. Do not discard the broccoli cooking water.

3 Add salt to the broccoli cooking water and bring back to the boil. Drop in the pasta, stir well, and cook until *al dente*.

4 While the pasta is boiling, heat the oil in a small saucepan. Add the garlic and, after 2–3 minutes, the anchovy fillets. Using a fork, mash the anchovies and garlic to a smooth paste. Then cook for a further 3–4 minutes.

5 Before draining the pasta, ladle 1–2 cupfuls of the cooking water over the broccoli. Add the drained pasta and the hot anchovy and oil mixture. Mix well, and season with salt and pepper if necessary. Serve at once.

Spaghetti with Eggs and Bacon

One of the classic pasta sauces, about which a debate still remains: whether or not it should contain cream. Pasta purists believe that it should not.

Serves 4

30ml/2 tbsp olive oil

150g/5oz bacon, cut into matchsticks

1 garlic clove, crushed

400g/14oz spaghetti

3 eggs, at room temperature

75g/3oz/¾ cup freshly grated
   Parmesan cheese

salt and ground black pepper

1 In a medium frying pan, heat the oil and sauté the bacon and the garlic until the bacon renders its fat and starts to brown. Remove and discard the garlic. Keep the bacon and its fat hot, until needed.

2 Cook the spaghetti in plenty of rapidly boiling salted water until *al dente*.

3 Meanwhile, warm a large serving bowl and break the eggs into it. Beat in the Parmesan cheese with a fork, and season with salt and pepper.

4 As soon as the pasta is done, drain it quickly, and mix it into the egg mixture. Pour on the hot bacon and its fat. Stir well. The heat from the pasta and bacon fat will lightly cook the beaten eggs. Serve immediately.

Rigatoni with Garlic Crumbs

A hot and spicy dish – halve the quantity of chilli if you like a milder flavour. The bacon is an optional addition; you can leave it out if you are cooking for vegetarians.

INGREDIENTS

Serves 4–6

45ml/3 tbsp olive oil

2 shallots, chopped

8 rashers streaky bacon, chopped (optional)

10ml/2 tsp crushed dried red chillies

400g/14oz can chopped tomatoes with garlic and herbs

6 slices white bread

115g/4oz/½ cup butter

2 garlic cloves, chopped

450g/1lb rigatoni

salt and ground black pepper

1 Heat the oil in a medium saucepan and fry the shallots and bacon, if using, gently for 6–8 minutes until golden. Add the dried chillies and chopped tomatoes, half-cover and simmer for 20 minutes.

2 Meanwhile, cut the crusts off the bread and discard them. Reduce the bread to crumbs in a blender or food processor.

3 Heat the butter in a frying pan, add the garlic and bread-crumbs and stir-fry until golden and crisp. (Don't let the crumbs catch and burn or the final result will be ruined.)

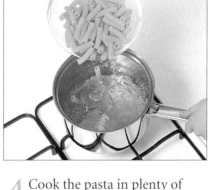

4 Cook the pasta in plenty of boiling salted water according to the instructions on the packet, until *al dente*. Drain well.

5 Toss the pasta with the tomato sauce and divide among four or six warmed serving plates.

6 Sprinkle with the crumbs and serve immediately.

Paglia e Fieno

The title of this dish translates as "straw and hay" which refers to the yellow and green colours of the pasta when mixed together. Fresh peas make all the difference to this dish.

INGREDIENTS

Serves 4

50g/2oz/4 tbsp butter

350g/12oz/3 cups frozen petits pois or 900g/2lb fresh peas, shelled

150ml/¼ pint/⅔ cup double cream, plus 60ml/4 tbsp extra

450g/1lb tagliatelle (plain and green mixed)

50g/2oz/½ cup freshly grated Parmesan cheese, plus extra to serve

freshly grated nutmeg

salt and ground black pepper

1 Melt the butter in a heavy saucepan and add the peas. Sauté for 2–3 minutes, then add the cream, bring to the boil and simmer for 1 minute until the mixture is slightly thickened.

2 Cook the plain and green mixed tagliatelle in plenty of boiling salted water according to the instructions on the packet, but for 2 minutes less time, until it is just *al dente*. Drain well and then turn into the saucepan containing the cream and pea sauce.

3 Place on the heat and turn the pasta in the sauce to coat. Pour in the extra cream, the cheese, salt and pepper to taste and a little grated nutmeg. Toss until well coated and heated through. Serve immediately with extra freshly grated Parmesan cheese.

COOK'S TIP

Sautéed mushrooms and narrow strips of cooked ham also make good additions to this dish.

Pasta Napoletana

The simple classic cooked tomato sauce with no adornments.

INGREDIENTS

Serves 4

900g/2lb fresh ripe red tomatoes or 750g/1¾lb canned plum tomatoes with their juice

1 onion, chopped

1 carrot, diced

1 celery stick, diced

150ml/¼ pint/⅔ cup dry white wine (optional)

1 sprig fresh parsley

pinch of caster sugar

15ml/1 tbsp chopped fresh oregano or 5ml/1 tsp dried

450g/1lb pasta, any variety

salt and ground black pepper

freshly grated Parmesan cheese, to serve

1 Roughly chop the tomatoes and place in a medium saucepan.

stirring occasionally. Strain, then stir in the oregano. Taste and adjust the seasoning if necessary.

2 Add all the other ingredients, except the oregano, pasta and cheese, and bring to the boil. Simmer, half-covered, for about 45 minutes until very thick,

3 Cook the pasta in plenty of boiling salted water according to the instructions on the packet, until *al dente*. Drain well.

4 Toss the pasta with the sauce. Serve with plenty of freshly grated Parmesan cheese.

Mushroom and Chilli Carbonara

*For a richer mushroom flavour, use
a small packet of dried Italian
porcini mushrooms in this quick
eggy sauce, and for an extra spicy
zing, toss in some chilli flakes too.*

INGREDIENTS

Serves 4

15g/½oz pack dried porcini mushrooms

300ml/½ pint/1¼ cups hot water

225g/8oz spaghetti

1 garlic clove, crushed

25g/1oz/2 tbsp butter

15ml/1 tbsp olive oil

225g/8oz button or chestnut mushrooms,
    thinly sliced

5ml/1 tsp dried red chilli flakes

2 eggs

300ml/½ pint/1¼ cups single cream

salt and ground black pepper

freshly grated Parmesan cheese and
    chopped fresh parsley, to serve

1 Soak the dried mushrooms in
the hot water for 15 minutes;
drain and reserve the liquor.

2 Cook the spaghetti according
to the instructions in plenty of
boiling salted water. Drain and
rinse in cold water.

3 In a large saucepan, lightly
sauté the garlic with the butter
and oil for half a minute.

4 Add the mushrooms,
including the soaked porcini
ones, and the chilli flakes, and stir
well. Cook for about 2 minutes.

5 Pour in the reserved soaking
liquor from the mushrooms
and boil the mixture to reduce
slightly.

6 Beat the eggs with the cream
and season well. Return the
cooked spaghetti to the pan and
toss in the eggs and cream. Reheat,
without boiling, and serve hot
sprinkled with grated Parmesan
cheese and chopped parsley.

VARIATION

Instead of mushrooms, try using
either finely sliced and sautéed
leeks or perhaps coarsely shredded
lettuce with peas. If chilli flakes are
too hot and spicy for you, then try
the delicious alternative of skinned
and chopped tomatoes with torn,
fresh basil leaves.

Tagliatelle with "Hit-the-pan" Salsa

It is possible to make a hot, filling meal within just 15 minutes with this quick-cook salsa sauce. If you have no time don't peel the tomatoes.

Serves 2

115g/4oz tagliatelle

45ml/3 tbsp olive oil, preferably
   extra virgin

3 large tomatoes

1 garlic clove, crushed

4 spring onions, sliced

1 green chilli, halved, seeded and sliced

juice of 1 orange (optional)

30ml/2 tbsp chopped fresh parsley

salt and ground black pepper

grated cheese, to serve (optional)

1 Cook the tagliatelle in plenty of boiling salted water until *al dente*. Drain and toss in a little of the oil. Season well.

2 Skin the tomatoes by dipping them in a bowl of boiling water for about 45 seconds and then into cold water. The skins should slip off easily. Roughly chop the flesh.

3 Heat the remaining oil until quite hot and stir-fry the garlic, onions and chilli for 1 minute.

4 Add the tomatoes, orange juice, if using, and parsley. Season well and stir in the tagliatelle to reheat. Serve with grated cheese, if desired.

> COOK'S TIP
>
> You could use any pasta shape for this recipe. It would be particularly good with large rigatoni or linguini, or as a sauce for fresh ravioli or tortellini.

Spaghetti with Garlic and Oil

This is one of the simplest and most satisfying pasta dishes of all. It is very popular throughout Italy. Use the best quality oil available for this splendid dish.

INGREDIENTS

Serves 4

400g/14oz spaghetti

90ml/6 tbsp extra virgin olive oil

3 garlic cloves, chopped

60ml/4 tbsp chopped fresh parsley

salt and ground black pepper

freshly grated Parmesan cheese, to
  serve (optional)

1 Cook the spaghetti in plenty of boiling salted water.

2 In a large frying pan heat the oil and gently sauté the garlic until barely golden. Do not let it brown or it will taste bitter. Stir in the chopped fresh parsley, then season with salt and pepper. Remove from the heat until the pasta is ready.

3 Drain the pasta when it is barely *al dente*. Tip it into the pan with the oil and garlic, and cook together for 2–3 minutes, stirring well to coat the spaghetti with the sauce. Serve at once in a warmed serving bowl, with some Parmesan cheese, if desired.

Spaghetti with Walnut Sauce

Like pesto, this sauce is traditionally ground in a pestle and mortar , but works just as well made in a blender or food processor. It is also good on tagliatelle and other pasta noodles.

INGREDIENTS

Serves 4

115g/4oz/1 cup walnut pieces or halves

45ml/3 tbsp plain breadcrumbs

45ml/3 tbsp olive or walnut oil

45ml/3 tbsp chopped fresh parsley

1–2 garlic cloves (optional)

50g/2oz/¼ cup butter, at room
  temperature

30ml/2 tbsp double cream

400g/14oz wholemeal spaghetti

salt and ground black pepper

freshly grated Parmesan cheese, to serve

1 Drop the nuts into a small pan of boiling water, and cook for 1–2 minutes. Drain, then skin. Dry on kitchen paper. Coarsely chop and set aside about a quarter.

2 Place the remaining nuts, the breadcrumbs, oil, parsley and garlic, if using, in a blender or food processor. Process to a paste. Remove to a bowl, and stir in the softened butter and the cream. Season with salt and pepper.

3 Cook the pasta in plenty of boiling salted water, following the instructions on the packet, until *al dente*. Drain, then toss with the sauce. Sprinkle with the reserved chopped nuts, and hand round the grated Parmesan separately.

Campanelle with Yellow Pepper Sauce

Roasted yellow peppers make a deliciously sweet and creamy sauce to serve with pasta.

INGREDIENTS

Serves 4

2 yellow peppers

50g/2oz/¼ cup soft goat's cheese

115g/4oz/½ cup low-fat fromage blanc

450g/1lb short pasta, such as campanelle or fusilli

salt and ground black pepper

50g/2oz/½ cup toasted flaked almonds, to serve

1 Place the whole yellow peppers under a preheated grill until charred and blistered. Place in a plastic bag, seal and leave to cool. Then peel and remove all the seeds.

2 Place the pepper flesh in a blender or food processor with the goat's cheese and fromage blanc. Process until smooth. Season with salt and plenty of ground black pepper.

3 Cook the pasta in plenty of boiling salted water, according to the instructions on the packet, until *al dente*. Drain well.

4 Toss with the sauce and serve sprinkled with the toasted flaked almonds.

Spaghetti with Olives and Mushrooms

A rich, pungent sauce topped with sweet cherry tomatoes.

Serves 4

15ml/1 tbsp olive oil

1 garlic clove, chopped

225g/8oz mushrooms, chopped

150g/5oz/scant 1 cup black olives, stoned

30ml/2 tbsp chopped fresh parsley

1 red chilli, seeded and chopped

450g/1lb spaghetti

225g/8oz cherry tomatoes

Parmesan cheese shavings, to
   serve (optional)

1 Heat the oil in a large pan. Add the garlic; cook for 1 minute. Add the chopped mushrooms, cover, and cook over a medium heat for 5 minutes.

2 Place the mushrooms in a blender or food processor with the olives, parsley and red chilli. Blend until smooth.

3 Cook the pasta in plenty of boiling salted water, according to the instructions on the packet, until *al dente*. Drain well and return to the pan. Add the olive mixture and toss together until the pasta is well coated. Cover and keep warm.

4 Heat an ungreased frying pan and shake the cherry tomatoes around until they start to split, about 2–3 minutes. Serve the pasta topped with the tomatoes and garnished with Parmesan cheese shavings, if desired.

Pasta with Spring Vegetables

Don't be tempted to use dried herbs in this flavoursome dish.

INGREDIENTS

Serves 4

115g/4oz broccoli florets

115g/4oz baby leeks

225g/8oz asparagus

1 small fennel bulb

115g/4oz/1 cup fresh or frozen peas

40g/1½oz/3 tbsp butter

1 shallot, chopped

45ml/3 tbsp chopped fresh mixed herbs, such as parsley, thyme and sage

300ml/½ pint/1¼ cups double cream

350g/12oz dried penne

salt and ground black pepper

freshly grated Parmesan cheese, to serve

1 Divide the broccoli florets into tiny sprigs. Cut the leeks and asparagus diagonally into 5cm/2in lengths. Trim the fennel bulb and remove any tough outer leaves. Cut into wedges, leaving the layers attached at the root ends so the pieces stay intact.

2 Cook each vegetable, including the peas, separately in boiling salted water until just tender – use the same water for each vegetable. Drain well and keep warm.

3 Melt the butter in a separate pan, add the chopped shallot and cook, stirring occasionally, until softened but not browned. Stir in the herbs and cream and cook for a few minutes, until slightly thickened.

4 Meanwhile, cook the pasta in plenty of boiling salted water for 10 minutes until *al dente*. Drain well and add to the sauce with the vegetables. Toss gently and season with plenty of pepper.

5 Serve the pasta hot with a sprinkling of freshly grated Parmesan cheese.

Tagliatelle with Spinach and Garlic Cheese

It's fun to mix ingredients from different cuisines and produce a delicious dish as a result. Italian pasta and spinach combine with Chinese soy sauce and French garlic-and-herb cream cheese to create this mouthwatering and wonderfully rich dish.

INGREDIENTS

Serves 4

225g/8oz tagliatelle, preferably
   mixed colours
225g/8oz fresh leaf spinach
30ml/2 tbsp light soy sauce
75g/3oz garlic-and-herb cheese
45ml/3 tbsp milk
salt and ground black pepper

1 Cook the tagliatelle in plenty of boiling salted water according to the instructions on the packet. Drain and return to the pan.

2 Blanch the spinach in a tiny amount of water until just wilted, then drain well, squeezing dry with the back of a wooden spoon. Chop roughly with scissors.

3 Return the spinach to its pan and stir in the soy sauce, garlic-and-herb cheese and milk. Bring slowly to the boil, stirring until smooth. Season to taste.

4 When the sauce is ready, pour over the pasta. Toss the pasta and sauce together and serve hot.

Spaghetti Olio e Aglio

This is a classic recipe from Rome. Originally the food of the poor, involving nothing more than pasta, olive oil (olio) and garlic (aglio), this is a quick and filling dish which is fast becoming fashionable the world over.

INGREDIENTS

Serves 4

2 garlic cloves

30ml/2 tbsp roughly chopped
    fresh parsley

120ml/4fl oz/½ cup olive oil

450g/1lb spaghetti

salt and ground black pepper

1 Using a sharp knife, peel and finely chop the two cloves of garlic.

2 Using a nylon chopping board and a sharp knife, roughly chop the fresh parsley.

3 Heat the olive oil in a medium saucepan and add the garlic and a pinch of salt. Cook gently, stirring all the time, until golden. If the garlic becomes too brown, it will taste bitter and spoil the dish.

4 Meanwhile cook the spaghetti in plenty of boiling salted water according to the instructions on the packet until *al dente*. Drain well through a colander.

5 Toss with the warm – not sizzling – garlic and oil and add plenty of black pepper and the parsley. Serve immediately.

Spaghetti with Fresh Tomato Sauce

The heat from the pasta will release the delicious flavours of this sauce. Only use the really red and soft tomatoes – large ripe beefsteak or Marmande tomatoes are ideal. Don't be tempted to use small hard tomatoes: they have very little flavour.

INGREDIENTS

Serves 4

4 large ripe tomatoes

2 garlic cloves, finely chopped

60ml/4 tbsp chopped fresh herbs, such as basil, marjoram, oregano or parsley

150ml/¼ pint/⅔ cup olive oil

450g/1lb spaghetti

salt and ground black pepper

1 Skin the tomatoes by placing in boiling water for 1 minute. Lift out with a slotted spoon and plunge into a bowl of cold water. Peel off the skins, then dry the tomatoes on kitchen paper.

2 Halve the tomatoes and squeeze out the seeds. Chop into 5mm/¼in cubes and mix with the garlic, herbs, olive oil and seasoning in a non-metallic bowl. Cover and allow the flavours to mellow for at least 30 minutes.

3 Cook the pasta in plenty of boiling salted water, according to the instructions on the packet.

4 Drain the pasta and mix with the sauce. Cover with a lid and leave for 2–3 minutes, then toss again and serve immediately.

VARIATION

Mix 115g/4oz/1 cup stoned and chopped black Greek olives into the sauce just before serving.

Tortellini with Cream, Butter and Cheese

This is an indulgent but quick alternative to macaroni cheese. Stir in some ham or pepperoni if you wish, though it's quite delicious as it is!

INGREDIENTS

Serves 4–6

450g/1lb fresh tortellini

50g/2oz/4 tbsp butter

300ml/½ pint/1¼ cups double cream

115g/4oz Parmesan cheese

freshly grated nutmeg

salt and ground black pepper

3 Grate the Parmesan cheese and stir 75g/3oz/¾ cup of it into the sauce until melted. Season to taste with salt, black pepper and nutmeg. Preheat the grill.

4 Drain the pasta well and spoon into a buttered heatproof serving dish. Pour over the sauce, sprinkle over the remaining cheese and place under the grill until brown and bubbling. Serve the tortellini immediately.

1 Cook the pasta in plenty of boiling salted water according to the instructions on the packet.

2 Meanwhile melt the butter in a medium saucepan and stir in the cream. Bring to the boil and cook for 2–3 minutes until the mixture is slightly thickened.

Greek Pasta with Avocado Sauce

This is an unusual sauce with a pale green colour, studded with red tomato. It has a luxurious, velvety texture. The sauce is rather rich, so you don't need too much of it.

INGREDIENTS

Serves 6

3 ripe tomatoes

2 large ripe avocados

25g/1oz/2 tbsp butter, plus extra for tossing the pasta

1 garlic clove, crushed

350ml/12fl oz/1½ cups double cream

dash of Tabasco sauce

450g/1lb green tagliatelle

salt and ground black pepper

freshly grated Parmesan cheese, to garnish

60ml/4 tbsp soured cream, to garnish

1 Halve the tomatoes and remove the cores. Squeeze out the seeds and dice the flesh. Set aside until required.

2 Halve the avocados, remove the stones and peel. Roughly chop the flesh. If hard-skinned, scoop out the flesh with a spoon.

3 Melt the butter in a saucepan and add the garlic. Cook for 1 minute, then add the cream and chopped avocados. Increase the heat, stirring constantly to break up the avocados.

4 Add the diced tomatoes and season to taste with salt, pepper and a little Tabasco sauce. Keep the mixture warm.

5 Cook the pasta in plenty of boiling salted water according to the instructions on the packet. Drain well through a colander and toss with a knob of butter.

6 Divide the pasta among four warmed bowls and spoon over the sauce. Sprinkle with grated Parmesan cheese and top with a spoonful of soured cream.

Pasta Shells with Tomatoes and Rocket

This pretty coloured pasta dish relies for its success on the salad green, rocket. Available in large supermarkets, it is a leaf easily grown in the garden or a window-box and tastes slightly peppery.

INGREDIENTS

Serves 4

450g/1lb pasta shells

450g/1lb ripe cherry tomatoes

75g/3oz fresh rocket leaves

45ml/3 tbsp olive oil

salt and ground black pepper

Parmesan cheese shavings, to serve

1 Cook the pasta in plenty of boiling salted water according to the instructions on the packet, until *al dente*. Drain well.

2 Halve the tomatoes. Trim, wash and dry the rocket leaves.

3 Heat the oil in a large saucepan, add the tomatoes and cook for barely 1 minute. The tomatoes should only just heat through and not disintegrate.

4 Add the pasta, then the rocket. Carefully stir to mix and heat through. Season well with salt and ground black pepper. Serve immediately with plenty of Parmesan cheese shavings.

Fettuccine all'Alfredo

A classic dish from Rome, Fettuccine all'Alfredo is simply pasta tossed with double cream, butter and freshly grated Parmesan cheese. Popular additions are peas and strips of ham.

INGREDIENTS

Serves 4

25g/1oz/2 tbsp butter

150ml/¼ pint/⅔ cup double cream, plus
   60ml/4 tbsp extra

450g/1lb fettuccine

50g/2oz/½ cup freshly grated Parmesan
   cheese, plus extra to serve

freshly grated nutmeg

salt and ground black pepper

1 Place the butter and 150ml/ ¼ pint/⅔ cup of the cream in a heavy saucepan, bring to the boil and simmer for 1 minute until slightly thickened.

2 Cook the fettuccine in plenty of boiling salted water according to the instructions on the packet, but for 2 minutes less time, until *al dente*.

3 Drain very well and turn into the pan with the cream sauce.

4 Place on the heat and turn the pasta in the sauce to coat thoroughly.

5 Add the extra 60ml/4 tbsp cream, the cheese, salt and pepper to taste and a little grated nutmeg. Toss until well coated and heated through. Serve at once with extra grated Parmesan cheese.

Linguine with Sweet Pepper and Cream

The sweetness of red onion complements the peppers in this dish.

Serves 4

1 orange pepper, cored, seeded and cubed

1 yellow pepper, cored, seeded and cubed

1 red pepper, cored, seeded and cubed

350g/12oz linguine

30ml/2 tbsp olive oil

1 red onion, sliced

1 garlic clove, chopped

30ml/2 tbsp chopped fresh rosemary

150ml/¼ pint/⅔ cup double cream

salt and ground black pepper

fresh rosemary sprigs, to garnish

5 Heat the oil in a frying pan and fry the onion and garlic for about 5 minutes until softened.

6 Stir in the sliced peppers and chopped rosemary and fry gently for about 5 minutes until heated through.

7 Stir in the cream and heat through gently. Season to taste with salt and pepper.

8 Drain the pasta thoroughly and toss in the sauce. Serve immediately, garnished with sprigs of fresh rosemary.

1 Preheat the grill to hot. Place the peppers, skin-side up, on a grill rack. Grill for 5–10 minutes until the skins begin to blister and char, turning occasionally.

2 Remove the peppers from the heat, cover with a clean dish towel and leave to stand for about 5 minutes.

3 Carefully peel away the skins from the peppers and discard. Slice the peppers into thin strips.

4 Cook the pasta in plenty of boiling salted water according to the instructions on the packet.

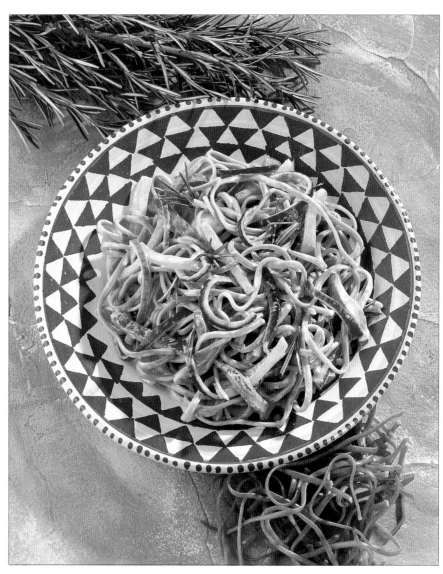

Piquant Chicken with Spaghetti

The addition of cucumber and tomatoes adds a deliciously fresh flavour to this unusual dish.

Serves 4

1 onion, finely chopped

1 carrot, diced

1 garlic clove, crushed

300ml/½ pint/1¼ cups vegetable stock

4 chicken breasts, boned and skinned

1 bouquet garni

115g/4oz button mushrooms, thinly sliced

5ml/1 tsp wine vinegar or lemon juice

350g/12oz spaghetti

½ cucumber, peeled and cut into fingers

2 tomatoes, skinned, seeded and chopped

30ml/2 tbsp crème fraîche

15ml/1 tbsp chopped fresh parsley

15ml/1 tbsp snipped chives

salt and ground black pepper

1 Put the onion, carrot, garlic, stock, chicken and bouquet garni into a saucepan.

2 Bring to the boil, cover and simmer for 15–20 minutes or until the chicken is tender. Transfer the chicken to a plate and cover with foil.

3 Remove the chicken and strain the liquid. Discard the vegetables and return the liquid to the pan. Add the sliced mushrooms, wine vinegar or lemon juice and simmer for 2–3 minutes.

4 Cook the spaghetti in plenty of boiling salted water according to the instructions on the packet. Drain thoroughly.

5 Blanch the cucumber in boiling water for 10 seconds. Drain and rinse under cold water.

6 Cut the chicken breasts into bite-size pieces. Boil the stock to reduce by half, then add the chicken, tomatoes, crème fraîche, cucumber and herbs. Season with salt and pepper to taste.

7 Transfer the spaghetti to a warmed serving dish and spoon over the piquant chicken. Serve at once.

Pasta Twists with Mushroom and Chorizo

The delicious combination of wild mushrooms and spicy sausage make this a tempting supper dish.

INGREDIENTS

Serves 4

350g/12oz pasta twists, such as cavatappi

60ml/4 tbsp olive oil

1 garlic clove, chopped

1 celery stick, chopped

225g/8oz chorizo sausage, sliced

225g/8oz mixed mushrooms, such as
   oyster, brown cap and shiitake

15ml/1 tbsp lemon juice

30ml/2 tbsp chopped fresh oregano

salt and ground black pepper

finely chopped fresh parsley, to garnish

1 Cook the pasta in plenty of boiling salted water according to the instructions on the packet.

2 Heat the oil in a frying pan and cook the garlic and celery for 5 minutes until the celery is softened but not browned.

COOK'S TIP

This dish is delicious served with lashings of Parmesan cheese shavings. Use any combination of mushrooms for this flavoursome sauce.

---

3 Add the chorizo and cook for 5 minutes, stirring from time to time, until browned.

4 Add the mushrooms and cook for a further 4 minutes, stirring from time to time, until they are slightly softened.

5 Stir in the remaining ingredients, and heat through.

6 Drain the pasta thoroughly and turn into a serving dish. Toss with the sauce to coat. Serve immediately, garnished with finely chopped fresh parsley.

Penne with Chicken and Ham Sauce

A meal in itself, this colourful pasta sauce is perfect for lunch or supper.

INGREDIENTS

Serves 4

350g/12oz penne
25g/1oz/2 tbsp butter
1 onion, chopped
1 garlic clove, chopped
1 bay leaf
450ml/¾ pint/1¾ cups dry white wine
150ml/¼ pint/⅔ cup crème fraîche
225g/8oz cooked chicken, skinned, boned
  and diced
115g/4oz cooked lean ham, diced
115g/4oz Gouda cheese, grated
15ml/1 tbsp chopped fresh mint
salt and ground black pepper
finely shredded fresh mint, to garnish

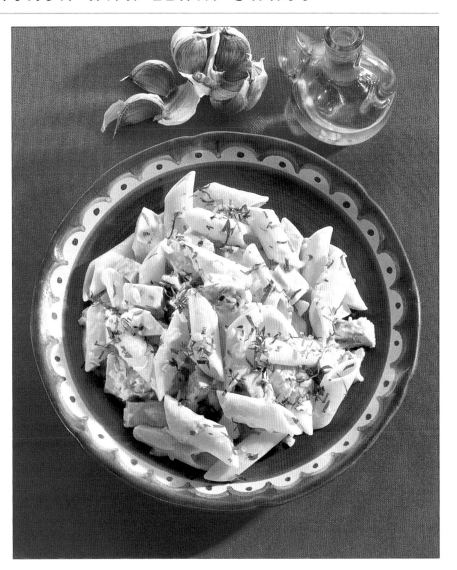

1 Cook the pasta in plenty of boiling salted water according to the instructions on the packet.

2 Heat the butter in a large frying pan and fry the onion for about 10 minutes, or until softened.

3 Add the garlic, bay leaf and wine and bring to the boil. Boil rapidly until reduced by about half. Remove the bay leaf, then stir in the crème fraîche and return to the boil.

4 Add the chicken, ham and Gouda cheese and simmer for 5 minutes, stirring occasionally until heated through.

5 Add the chopped fresh mint and season to taste.

6 Drain the pasta thoroughly and turn it into a large serving dish. Toss with the sauce, garnish with finely shredded fresh mint and serve immediately.

Tagliatelle with Peas, Asparagus and Beans

A creamy pea sauce makes a wonderful combination with crunchy young vegetables.

Serves 4

15ml/1 tbsp olive oil

1 garlic clove, crushed

6 spring onions, sliced

225g/8oz/2 cups frozen peas, thawed

350g/12oz fresh young asparagus

30ml/2 tbsp chopped fresh sage, plus extra leaves to garnish

finely grated rind of 2 lemons

450ml/¾ pint/1¾ cups vegetable stock or water

225g/8oz/2 cups frozen broad beans, thawed

450g/1lb tagliatelle

60ml/4 tbsp low-fat natural yogurt

1 Heat the oil in a pan. Add the garlic and spring onions and cook gently for 2–3 minutes.

2 Add the peas and 115g/4oz of the asparagus, together with the sage, lemon rind and stock or water. Bring to the boil, reduce the heat and simmer for 10 minutes until tender. Purée in a blender or food processor until smooth.

3 Meanwhile remove the outer skins from the thawed broad beans and discard.

4 Cut the remaining asparagus into 5cm/2in lengths, trimming off any fibrous stems, and blanch in boiling water for 2 minutes.

5 Cook the tagliatelle in plenty of boiling salted water according to the instructions on the packet until *al dente*. Drain well.

6 Add the cooked asparagus and shelled beans to the sauce and reheat. Stir in the yogurt and toss into the tagliatelle. Garnish with sage leaves and serve at once.

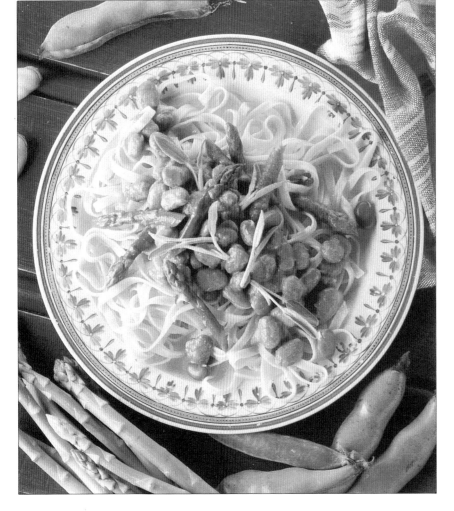

Rigatoni with Scallop Sauce

A jewel from the sea, the scallop is what makes this sauce so special. Serve with a green salad, if liked.

INGREDIENTS

Serves 4

350g/12oz rigatoni

350g/12oz queen scallops

45ml/3 tbsp olive oil

1 garlic clove, chopped

1 onion, chopped

2 carrots, cut into matchsticks

30 ml/2 tbsp chopped fresh parsley

30ml/2 tbsp dry white wine

30ml/2 tbsp Pernod

150ml/¼ pint/⅔ cup double cream

salt and ground black pepper

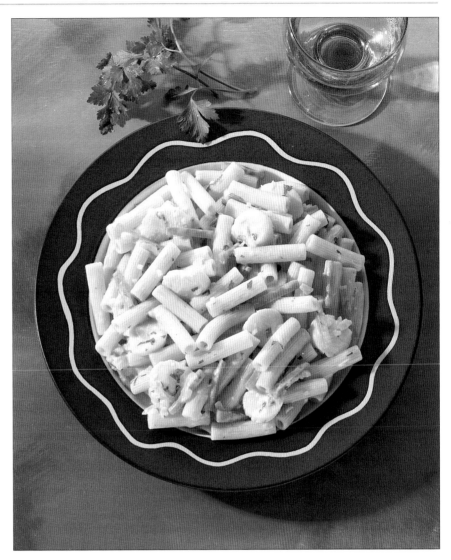

1 Cook the pasta in plenty of boiling salted water according to the instructions on the packet.

2 Trim the scallops, separating the corals from the white eye part of the meat.

3 Using a sharp knife, cut the eye in half lengthways.

4 Heat the oil in a frying pan and fry the garlic, onion and carrots for 5–10 minutes until the carrots are softened.

5 Stir in the scallops, parsley, wine and Pernod and bring to the boil. Cover and simmer for about 1 minute. Using a slotted spoon, transfer the scallops and vegetables to a plate and keep them warm until required.

6 Bring the pan juices back to the boil and boil rapidly until reduced by half. Stir in the cream and heat the sauce through.

7 Return the scallops and vegetables to the pan and heat them through. Season to taste.

8 Drain the pasta thoroughly and toss with the sauce. Serve the rigatoni immediately.

Tagliatelle with Hazelnut Pesto

Hazelnuts provide an interesting alternative to pine nuts in this delicious pesto sauce.

INGREDIENTS

Serves 4

2 garlic cloves, crushed

25g/1oz/1 cup fresh basil leaves

25g/1oz/¼ cup hazelnuts

200g/7oz/scant 1 cup skimmed milk
   soft cheese

225g/8oz dried tagliatelle, or
   450g/1lb fresh

salt and ground black pepper

1 Place the garlic, basil, hazelnuts and cheese in a blender or food processor and process to form a thick paste.

2 Cook the tagliatelle in plenty of lightly salted boiling water according to the instructions on the packet until just tender, then drain thoroughly.

3 Spoon the sauce into the hot pasta, tossing until melted. Sprinkle with ground black pepper to taste and serve hot.

Spaghetti with Tuna Sauce

A speedy midweek meal, which can also be made with other pasta shapes, for a change.

INGREDIENTS

Serves 4

225g/8oz dried spaghetti, or
   450g/1lb fresh

1 garlic clove, crushed

400g/14oz can chopped tomatoes

425g/15oz can tuna fish in brine, flaked

2.5ml/½ tsp chilli sauce (optional)

4 stoned black olives, chopped

salt and ground black pepper

1 Cook the spaghetti in plenty of lightly salted boiling water, according to the instructions on the packet, or until *al dente*. Drain well and keep hot until required.

2 Place the garlic and tomatoes in the saucepan and bring to the boil. Simmer, uncovered, for about 2–3 minutes.

3 Add the tuna, chilli sauce, if using, the olives and spaghetti. Heat well, add the seasoning to taste and serve hot.

COOK'S TIP

~

If fresh tuna is available, use 450g/1lb cut into small chunks, and add after step 2. Simmer for 6–8 minutes, then add the chilli, olives and pasta.

Pasta with Pesto Sauce

Don't stint on the fresh basil – this is the most wonderful sauce in the world! And it tastes completely different from the ready-made pesto sold in jars.

INGREDIENTS

Serves 4

2 garlic cloves

50g/2oz/½ cup pine nuts

40g/1½oz/1 cup fresh basil leaves

150ml/¼ pint/⅔ cup olive oil

50g/2oz/4 tbsp unsalted butter, softened

60ml/4 tbsp freshly grated
   Parmesan cheese

450g/1lb spaghetti

salt and ground black pepper

1 Peel the garlic and process in a blender or food processor with a little salt and the pine nuts until broken up. Add the basil leaves and continue mixing to a paste.

2 Gradually add the olive oil, little by little, until the mixture is creamy and thick.

3 Beat in the butter and season with ground black pepper. Beat in the cheese. Alternatively, you can make the pesto by hand using a pestle and mortar.

4 Store the pesto sauce in a jar, with a layer of olive oil on top to exclude the air, in the fridge until needed.

5 Cook the pasta in plenty of boiling salted water according to the instructions on the packet, until *al dente*. Drain well.

6 Toss the pasta with half the pesto and serve in warm bowls, with the remaining pesto sauce spooned over the top.

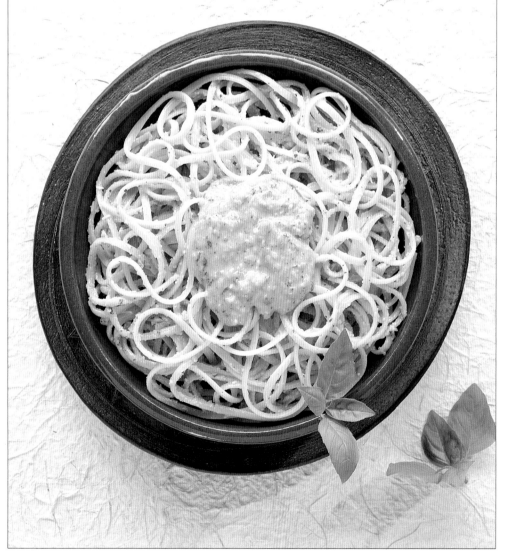

Spaghetti with Feta Cheese

We think of pasta as being essentially Italian but, in fact, the Greeks have a great appetite for it too. It complements tangy, full-flavoured feta cheese beautifully in this simple but effective dish.

INGREDIENTS

Serves 2–3

115g/4oz spaghetti

1 garlic clove

30ml/2 tbsp extra virgin olive oil

8 cherry tomatoes, halved

a little freshly grated nutmeg

salt and ground black pepper

75g/3oz feta cheese, crumbled

15ml/1 tbsp chopped fresh basil

a few black olives, to serve (optional)

1 Cook the spaghetti in plenty of boiling salted water according to the instructions on the packet, then drain well.

2 In the same pan gently heat the garlic clove in the olive oil for 1–2 minutes, then add the halved cherry tomatoes.

3 Increase the heat to fry the tomatoes lightly for 1 minute, then remove the garlic and discard.

4 Toss in the spaghetti, season with the nutmeg and salt and pepper to taste, then stir in the crumbled feta cheese and basil.

5 Check the seasoning, remembering that feta can be quite salty, and serve hot topped with black olives, if desired.

SIMPLE
SUPPERS

Tortelli with Pumpkin Stuffing

During autumn and winter the northern Italian markets are full of bright orange pumpkins which are used to make soups and pasta dishes. This flavoursome dish is a speciality of Mantua.

INGREDIENTS

Serves 6-8

1kg/2¼lb pumpkin (weight with shell)
75g/3oz/1½ cups amaretti
   biscuits, crushed
2 eggs
75g/3oz/¾ cup freshly grated
   Parmesan cheese
pinch of grated nutmeg
plain breadcrumbs, as required
egg pasta sheets made with 3 eggs
salt and ground black pepper

To serve
115g/4oz/½ cup butter
75g/3oz/¾ cup freshly grated
   Parmesan cheese

1 Preheat the oven to 190°C/375°F/Gas 5. Then cut the pumpkin into 10cm/4in pieces, leaving the skin on. Place the pumpkin pieces in a covered casserole and bake for about 45–50 minutes. When cool, cut off the skins. Purée the flesh in a food mill, blender or food processor or press through a sieve with a wooden spoon.

2 Combine the pumpkin purée with the biscuit crumbs, eggs, Parmesan and nutmeg. Season with salt and pepper. If the mixture is too wet, add about 15–30ml/1–2 tbsp breadcrumbs. Set aside until required.

3 Prepare the sheets of egg pasta. Roll out very thinly by hand or machine. Do not let the pasta dry out before filling.

4 Place tablespoonfuls of filling every 6cm/2½in along the pasta in rows 5cm/2in apart. Cover with another sheet of pasta, and press down gently. Use a fluted pastry or pasta wheel to cut between the rows to form rectangles with filling in the centre of each. Place the tortelli on a lightly floured surface, and allow to dry for at least 30 minutes, turning occasionally to dry both sides.

5 Bring a large pan of salted water to the boil. Gently heat the butter over a very low heat, taking care that it does not darken.

6 Drop the tortelli into the boiling water. Stir to prevent them from sticking. They will be cooked in 4–5 minutes. Drain and arrange in individual dishes. Spoon over the melted butter, sprinkle with grated Parmesan cheese and serve at once.

Stuffed Pasta Half-moons

These stuffed egg pasta half-moons are filled with a delicate mixture of cheeses. They make an elegant first course as well as a good supper.

INGREDIENTS

Serves 6–8

225g/8oz/1¼ cups fresh ricotta or
   curd cheese
225g/8oz/1¼ cups mozzarella cheese
115g/4oz/1 cup freshly grated
   Parmesan cheese
2 eggs
45ml/3 tbsp finely chopped fresh basil
salt and ground black pepper
egg pasta sheets made with 3 eggs

For the sauce
450g/1lb fresh tomatoes
30ml/2 tbsp olive oil
1 small onion, very finely chopped
90ml/6 tbsp cream

1 Press the ricotta or curd cheese through a sieve or strainer. Chop the mozzarella into very small cubes. Combine all three cheeses in a bowl. Beat in the eggs and basil, season and set aside.

2 Make the sauce by dropping the tomatoes into a small pan of boiling water for 1 minute. Remove, and peel using a small sharp knife to pull off the skins. Chop the tomatoes finely. Heat the oil in a medium saucepan. Add the onion and cook over a moderate heat until soft and translucent. Add the tomatoes and cook until soft, about 15 minutes. Season with salt and pepper. (The sauce may be pressed through a sieve to make it smooth.) Set aside.

3 Prepare the sheets of egg pasta. Roll out very thinly by hand or machine. Do not let the pasta dry out before filling.

4 Using a glass or pastry cutter, cut out rounds approximately 10cm/4in in diameter. Spoon one large tablespoon of the cheese filling on to one half of each pasta round and fold over.

5 Press the edges closed with a fork. Re-roll any trimmings and use to make more rounds. Allow the half-moons to dry for at least 10–15 minutes. Turn them over so they dry evenly.

6 Bring a large pan of salted water to the boil. Meanwhile, place the tomato sauce in a small saucepan and heat gently. Stir in the cream. Do not allow to boil.

7 Gently drop in the stuffed pasta, and stir carefully to prevent them from sticking. Cook for 5–7 minutes. Scoop them out of the water, drain carefully, and arrange in individual dishes. Spoon on some sauce to serve.

Baked Vegetable Lasagne

Following the principles of the classic meat sauce lasagne, other combinations of ingredients can be used most effectively. This vegetarian lasagne uses tomatoes and wild and cultivated mushrooms.

INGREDIENTS

Serves 8

egg pasta sheets made with 3 eggs

30ml/2 tbsp olive oil

1 onion, very finely chopped

500g/1¼lb tomatoes, fresh or
   canned, chopped

salt and ground black pepper

675g/1½lb cultivated or wild mushrooms,
   or a combination of both

75g/3oz/⅓ cup butter

2 garlic cloves, finely chopped

juice of ½ lemon

1 litre/1¾ pints/4 cups béchamel sauce

175g/6oz/1½ cups freshly grated
   Parmesan or Cheddar cheese, or a
   combination of both

1 Butter a large shallow baking dish, preferably rectangular or square in shape.

2 Make the egg pasta. Do not let it dry out before cutting into rectangles measuring about 11cm/4½in wide and the same length as the baking dish (this will make it easier to assemble).

3 In a small frying pan heat the oil and sauté the onion until translucent. Add the chopped tomatoes and cook for about 6–8 minutes, stirring often. Season with salt and pepper and set aside until required.

4 Wipe the mushrooms carefully with a damp cloth. Slice finely. Heat 40g/1½oz/3 tbsp of the butter in a frying pan and, when it is bubbling, add the mushrooms. Cook until the mushrooms start to exude their juices. Add the garlic and lemon juice, and season with salt and pepper. Cook until the liquids have almost all evaporated and the mushrooms are starting to brown. Set aside.

5 Preheat the oven to 200°C/ 400°F/Gas 6. Bring a very large pan of water to the boil. Place a large bowl of cold water near the cooker. Cover a large work surface with a tablecloth. Add salt to the rapidly boiling water. Drop in three or four of the egg pasta rectangles. Cook very briefly, about 30 seconds. Remove from the pan using a slotted spoon and then drop into the cold water for about 30 seconds. Remove and lay out to dry. Continue with the remaining pasta.

6 To assemble the lasagne, spread one large spoonful of the béchamel sauce over the base of the dish. Arrange a layer of pasta in the dish, cutting it with a sharp knife to fit. Cover with a thin layer of mushrooms, then one of béchamel sauce. Sprinkle with a little cheese.

7 Make another layer of pasta, spread with a thin layer of tomatoes, and then one of béchamel. Sprinkle with cheese. Repeat the layers in the same order, ending with a layer of pasta coated with béchamel. Do not make more than about six layers of pasta. Use the pasta trimmings to patch any gaps in the pasta. Sprinkle with more cheese and dot with butter.

8 Bake for 20 minutes. Remove from the oven and allow to stand for 5 minutes before serving.

Ravioli with Ricotta and Spinach

Home-made ravioli are fun to make and can be stuffed with different meat, cheese or vegetable fillings. This filling is easy to make and lighter than the more normal meat variety.

INGREDIENTS

Serves 4

400g/14oz fresh spinach or 175g/6oz
   frozen spinach
175g/6oz/¾ cup ricotta cheese
1 egg
50g/2oz/½ cup grated Parmesan cheese
pinch of grated nutmeg
egg pasta sheets made with 3 eggs
salt and ground black pepper

For the sauce
75g/3oz/⅓ cup butter
5–6 fresh sage sprigs

1 If using fresh spinach wash well in several changes of water. Place in a saucepan with only the water that is clinging to the leaves. Cover and cook until tender, about 5 minutes, then drain. Cook frozen spinach according to the instructions on the packet. When the spinach is cool, squeeze out as much moisture as possible then chop the leaves finely.

2 Combine the chopped spinach with the ricotta, egg, Parmesan and nutmeg. Mix well. Season with salt and pepper. Cover the bowl and set aside.

3 Prepare the sheets of egg pasta. Roll out very thinly by hand or machine. Do not let the pasta dry out before filling.

4 Place small teaspoonfuls of filling along the pasta in rows 5cm/2in apart. Cover with another sheet of pasta, pressing down gently to avoid forming any air pockets inside the ravioli.

5 Use a fluted pastry or pasta wheel to cut between the rows to form small squares with filling in the centre of each. If the edges do not stick well, moisten with milk or water and press together with a fork. Place the ravioli on a lightly floured surface, and allow to dry for at least 30 minutes, turning occasionally. Bring a large pan of salted water to the boil.

6 Heat the butter and sage together over a very low heat, taking care that the butter does not darken at all.

7 Drop the ravioli into the boiling water. Stir gently to prevent them from sticking. They will be cooked in very little time, about 4–5 minutes. Drain carefully and arrange in individual serving dishes. Spoon over the sauce and serve at once.

Baked Macaroni with Cheese

This delicious dish is perhaps less common in Italy than other pasta dishes, but has become a family favourite around the world.

INGREDIENTS

Serves 6

475ml/16fl oz/2 cups milk

1 bay leaf

3 mace blades or pinch of grated nutmeg

50g/2oz/4 tbsp butter

40g/1½oz/⅓ cup flour

175g/6oz/1½ cups grated Parmesan or
   Cheddar cheese, or a combination
   of both

40g/½oz/1/3 cup breadcrumbs

450g/1lb macaroni or other short
   hollow pasta

salt and ground black pepper

1 Make a béchamel sauce by gently heating the milk with the bay leaf and mace, if using, in a small saucepan. Do not let it boil. Melt the butter in a medium, heavy-based saucepan. Add the flour, and mix it in well with a wire whisk. Cook for 2–3 minutes, but do not let the butter burn. Strain the hot milk into the flour and butter mixture all at once, and mix smoothly with the whisk. Bring the sauce to the boil, stirring constantly, and cook for a further 4–5 minutes.

2 Season with salt and pepper, and the nutmeg if no mace has been used. Add all but 30ml/2 tbsp of the cheese, and stir over a low heat until melted. Place a layer of clear film right on the surface of the sauce to prevent a skin forming and set aside.

3 Preheat the oven to 200°C/ 400°F/Gas 6. Grease an ovenproof dish and sprinkle with some breadcrumbs. Cook the pasta in plenty of boiling salted water until *al dente*.

4 Drain the pasta, and combine it with the sauce. Pour it into the prepared dish. Sprinkle the top with the remaining breadcrumbs and grated cheese and bake in the centre of the oven for 20 minutes, until golden and bubbling.

Pasta with Roasted Pepper and Tomato

Add other vegetables such as French beans or courgettes or even chick-peas to make this sauce more substantial, if you like.

INGREDIENTS

Serves 4

2 red peppers

2 yellow peppers

45ml/3 tbsp olive oil

1 onion, sliced

2 garlic cloves, crushed

2.5ml/½ tsp mild chilli powder

400g/14oz can chopped tomatoes

450g/1lb dried pasta shells or spirals

salt and ground black pepper

freshly grated Parmesan cheese, to serve

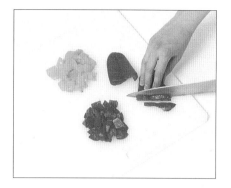

1 Preheat the oven to 200°C/400°/Gas 6. Place the peppers on a baking sheet or in a roasting tin and bake for about 20 minutes or until they are beginning to char. Alternatively you could grill the peppers, turning frequently until evenly blistered.

2 Rub the skins off the peppers under cold water. Halve, seed and roughly chop the flesh.

3 Heat the oil in a medium saucepan and add the onion and garlic. Cook gently for 5 minutes until soft and golden.

4 Stir in the chilli powder, cook for 2 minutes, then add the tomatoes and peppers. Bring to the boil and simmer for 10–15 minutes until the sauce is slightly thickened and reduced. Season.

5 Cook the pasta in plenty of boiling salted water according to the instructions on the packet. Drain well and toss with the sauce. Serve piping hot with plenty of grated Parmesan cheese.

Tagliatelle with Walnut Sauce

An unusual sauce which would make this a spectacular dinner party starter or satisfying supper.

INGREDIENTS

Serves 4–6

2 thick slices wholemeal bread

300ml/½ pint/1¼ cups milk

275g/10oz/2½ cups walnut pieces

1 garlic clove, crushed

50g/2oz/½ cup freshly grated
Parmesan cheese

90ml/6 tbsp olive oil, plus extra for
tossing the pasta

150ml/¼ pint/⅔ cup double
cream (optional)

450g/1lb tagliatelle

salt and ground black pepper

30ml/2 tbsp chopped fresh parsley,
to garnish

3 Place the bread, walnuts, garlic, Parmesan cheese and olive oil in a blender or food processor and blend until smooth. Season to taste with salt and pepper. Stir in the cream, if using.

4 Cook the pasta in plenty of boiling salted water according to the instructions on the packet, drain and toss with a little olive oil. Divide the pasta equally among four or six bowls and place a dollop of sauce on each portion. Sprinkle with parsley.

1 Cut the crusts off the bread and soak in the milk until all of the milk is absorbed.

2 Preheat the oven to 190°C/ 375°F/Gas 5. Spread the walnuts on a baking sheet and toast in the oven for 5 minutes. Leave to cool.

Fusilli with Peppers and Onions

Peppers are characteristic of southern Italy. When grilled and peeled they have a delicious smoky flavour, and are easier to digest.

INGREDIENTS

Serves 4

450g/1lb red and yellow peppers
90ml/6 tbsp olive oil
1 large red onion, thinly sliced
2 garlic cloves, minced
400g/14oz fusilli or other short pasta
45ml/3 tbsp finely chopped fresh parsley
salt and ground black pepper
freshly grated Parmesan cheese, to serve

1 Place the peppers under a hot grill and turn occasionally until they are blackened and blistered on all sides. Remove from the heat, place in a plastic bag, seal and leave for 5 minutes.

2 Peel the peppers. Cut them into quarters, remove the stems and seeds, and slice into thin strips.

3 Heat the oil in a large frying pan. Add the onion, and cook over a moderate heat until translucent, 5–8 minutes. Stir in the garlic, and cook for a further 2 minutes.

4 Cook the pasta in plenty of boiling salted water until just *al dente*. Do not drain yet.

5 Meanwhile, add the peppers to the onion, and mix together gently. Stir in about 45ml/3 tbsp of the pasta cooking water. Season with salt and pepper. Stir in the finely chopped fresh parsley.

6 Drain the pasta. Tip it into the pan with the vegetables, and cook over a moderate heat for 3–4 minutes, stirring constantly to mix the pasta into the sauce. Serve with the grated Parmesan cheese handed round separately.

Ravioli with Cheese and Herbs

Vary the herbs according to what you have to hand.

INGREDIENTS

Serves 4–6

225g/8oz/1 cup full-fat soft
   cheese, softened

1 garlic clove, finely chopped

25g/1oz mixed herbs, such as thyme, basil,
   chives and parsley, finely chopped

1 quantity fresh pasta dough, rolled by
   machine into 2 x 30cm/12in strips, or
   divided into 4 and rolled by hand as
   thinly as possible

semolina, to coat

115g/4oz/½ cup butter

salt and ground black pepper

1 Mix together the soft cheese, garlic and most of the herbs. Season with salt and pepper.

2 Make the ravioli, filling them with the cheese and herb mixture. Toss the ravioli in a little semolina to coat lightly and leave to rest at room temperature for about 15 minutes.

3 Bring a large pan of salted water to the boil. Drop in the ravioli and cook for 7–9 minutes or until they are just tender to the bite. Drain well.

4 Melt the butter. Toss the ravioli in the melted butter. Sprinkle with the remaining herbs and serve immediately.

VARIATION

For Ravioli with Gorgonzola and Pine Nuts, fill the ravioli with a mixture of 115g/4oz/½ cup each full-fat soft cheese and crumbled Gorgonzola cheese; omit the garlic and herbs. Sprinkle the cooked ravioli with 25g/1oz/¼ cup toasted pine nuts instead of herbs.

Pasta with Courgette and Walnut Sauce

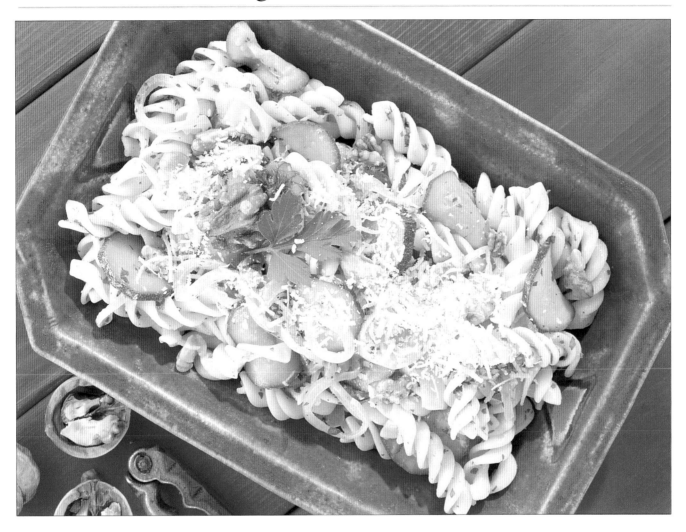

The vegetables are softened slowly to release their flavours.

INGREDIENTS

Serves 4

65g/2½oz/5 tbsp butter

1 large Spanish onion, halved and
    thinly sliced

450g/1lb courgettes, very thinly sliced

375g/12oz short pasta shapes, such as
    penne, ziti, rotini or fusilli

50g/2oz/½ cup walnuts, coarsely chopped

45ml/3 tbsp chopped fresh parsley

30ml/2 tbsp single cream

salt and ground black pepper

freshly grated Parmesan cheese, to serve

1 Melt the butter in a frying pan. Add the onion, cover and sweat for 5 minutes until translucent, then add the courgettes.

2 Stir well, cover again and sweat until the vegetables are very soft, stirring occasionally.

3 Meanwhile, cook the pasta in plenty of boiling salted water, according to the instructions on the packet, until *al dente*.

4 While the pasta is cooking, add the walnuts, parsley and cream to the courgette mixture and stir well. Season with salt and pepper.

5 Drain the pasta and return to the pan. Add the courgette sauce and mix together well. Serve immediately, with freshly grated Parmesan to sprinkle over.

Penne with Broccoli and Chilli

For a milder flavour, remove the seeds from the chilli.

INGREDIENTS

Serves 4

350g/12oz penne

450g/1lb small broccoli florets

30ml/2 tbsp stock

1 garlic clove, crushed

1 small red chilli, sliced,
  or 2.5ml/½ tsp chilli sauce

60ml/4 tbsp natural low-fat yogurt

30ml/2 tbsp toasted pine nuts or
  cashew nuts

salt and ground black pepper

1 Add the pasta to a large pan of lightly salted boiling water and return to the boil. Then place the broccoli in a steamer basket over the top. Cover and cook for about 8–10 minutes until both are just tender. Drain well.

2 Heat the stock and add the crushed garlic and chilli or chilli sauce. Stir over a low heat for 2–3 minutes.

3 Stir in the broccoli, pasta and yogurt. Adjust the seasoning, sprinkle with nuts and serve hot.

Spaghetti with Meatballs

*No Italian menu would be complete
without meatballs. Serve these with
a light green salad if you like.*

INGREDIENTS

Serves 4

For the meatballs

1 onion, chopped

1 garlic clove, chopped

350g/12oz/3 cups minced lamb

1 egg yolk

15ml/1 tbsp dried mixed herbs

15ml/1 tbsp olive oil

salt and ground black pepper

For the sauce

300ml/½ pint/1¼ cups passata

30ml/2 tbsp chopped fresh basil

1 garlic clove, chopped

salt and ground black pepper

350g/12oz spaghetti

fresh rosemary sprigs, to garnish

freshly grated Parmesan cheese, to serve

1 To make the meatballs, mix together the onion, garlic, lamb, egg yolk, herbs and seasoning until well blended.

2 Divide the mixture into about 20 pieces and mould into balls. Place on a baking sheet, cover with clear film and chill for at least 30 minutes.

3 Heat the oil in a large frying pan and add the meatballs. Fry for about 10 minutes, turning occasionally, until browned.

4 Add the passata, basil, garlic and seasoning to the pan and bring to the boil. Cover and simmer for 20 minutes, or until the meatballs are tender.

5 Meanwhile, cook the pasta in plenty of boiling salted water according to the instructions on the packet. Drain thoroughly and divide among four serving plates. Spoon over the meatballs and some of the sauce. Garnish each portion with a fresh rosemary sprig and serve immediately with plenty of freshly grated Parmesan cheese handed separately.

Pasta Salade Tiède

Boil a pan of pasta shapes and toss with vinaigrette dressing and some freshly prepared salad vegetables and you have the basis for a delicious warm salad.

INGREDIENTS

Serves 2

115g/4oz pasta shapes, such as shells

45ml/3 tbsp vinaigrette dressing

3 sun-dried tomatoes in oil, chopped

2 spring onions, sliced

25g/1oz watercress or rocket, chopped

¼ cucumber, halved, seeded and sliced

salt and ground black pepper

about 40g/1½oz pecorino cheese,
   coarsely grated, to garnish

1 Cook the pasta in plenty of boiling salted water according to the instructions on the packet. Drain and toss in the dressing.

2 Mix in the tomatoes, onions, watercress or rocket and cucumber. Season to taste.

3 Divide between two plates and sprinkle over the cheese. Serve at room temperature.

Penne with "Can-can" Sauce

The quality of canned pulses and tomatoes is so good that it is possible to transform them into a very fresh-tasting pasta sauce in minutes. Choose whatever pasta you like.

INGREDIENTS

Serves 3–4

225g/8oz penne

1 onion, sliced

1 red pepper, seeded and sliced

30ml/2 tbsp olive oil

400g/14oz chopped tomatoes

425g/15oz can chick-peas

30ml/2 tbsp dry vermouth (optional)

5ml/1 tsp dried oregano

1 large bay leaf

30ml/2 tbsp capers

salt and ground black pepper

1 Cook the pasta in plenty of boiling salted water according to the instructions on the packet, then drain. In a saucepan, gently fry the onion and pepper in the oil for about 5 minutes, stirring occasionally, until softened.

2 Add the tomatoes, chick-peas with their liquor, vermouth, if using, herbs and capers.

3 Season and bring to the boil, then simmer the mixture for about 10 minutes. Remove the bay leaf and mix in the pasta, reheat and serve hot.

Spaghetti with Tomato Sauce

Don't be put off by the idea of anchovies, they give a wonderful richness to the sauce, without adding their usual salty flavour.

INGREDIENTS

Serves 4

45ml/3 tbsp olive oil

1 onion, chopped

1 large garlic clove, chopped

400g/14oz can of chopped tomatoes
    with herbs

60ml/4 tbsp dry white wine

350g/12oz dried spaghetti

5–10ml/1–2 tsp dark soft brown sugar

50g/2oz can anchovy fillets in oil

115g/4oz pepperoni sausage, chopped

15ml/1 tbsp chopped fresh basil

salt and ground black pepper

sprigs of basil, to garnish

1 Heat the oil in a saucepan and fry the onion and garlic for 2 minutes to soften. Add the tomatoes and wine, bring to the boil and leave to simmer gently for 10–15 minutes. Put the pasta on to cook as directed.

2 After the sauce has been cooking 10 minutes add the soft brown sugar and the anchovy fillets, drained and chopped. Mix well and cook for about a further 5 minutes or so.

3 Drain the pasta and toss in very little oil. Add to it the pepperoni and the basil and sprinkle with seasoning. Serve topped with the tomato sauce and garnish with the sprigs of basil.

Tortellini with Cheese Sauce

Here is a very quick way of making a delicious cheese sauce without all the usual effort. But do eat it when really hot before the sauce starts to thicken. Blue cheese would work just as well, for a change.

INGREDIENTS

Serves 4

450g/1lb fresh tortellini

115g/4oz/½ cup ricotta or cream cheese

60–90ml/4-6 tbsp milk

50g/2oz/½ cup St Paulin or mozzarella
    cheese, grated

50g/2oz/½ cup Parmesan cheese, grated

2 garlic cloves, crushed

30ml/2 tbsp chopped, mixed fresh herbs,
    such as parsley, chives, basil or oregano

salt and ground black pepper

1 Cook the pasta according to the packet instructions, in boiling, salted water, stirring occasionally.

2 Meanwhile, gently melt the ricotta or cream cheese with the milk in a large pan. When blended, stir in the St Paulin or mozzarella, half the Parmesan, and the garlic and herbs.

3 Drain the cooked pasta and add to the pan of sauce. Stir well, and allow to cook gently for 1–2 minutes so the cheeses melt well. Season to taste and serve with the remaining Parmesan cheese sprinkled on top.

Spaghetti with Aubergine and Tomato

A great supper recipe – serve this aubergine and tomato dish with freshly cooked mange-touts.

INGREDIENTS

Serves 4

3 small aubergines

olive oil, for frying

450g/1lb spaghetti

1 quantity Classic Tomato Sauce
  (see Curly Lasagne with Classic
  Tomato Sauce)

225g/8oz fontina cheese, grated

salt and ground black pepper

1 Top and tail the aubergines and slice thinly. Arrange in a colander, sprinkling with plenty of salt between each layer. Leave to stand for about 30 minutes.

2 Rinse the aubergines under cold running water. Drain and pat dry on kitchen paper.

3 Heat plenty of oil in a large frying pan and fry the aubergine slices in batches for about 5 minutes, turning them once during the cooking time, until evenly browned.

4 Meanwhile, cook the pasta in plenty of boiling salted water according to the instructions on the packet, until *al dente*.

5 Stir the tomato sauce into the pan with the aubergines and bring to the boil. Cover and then simmer for 5 minutes.

6 Stir in the fontina cheese and salt and pepper. Continue stirring over a medium heat until the cheese melts.

7 Drain the pasta and stir into the sauce, tossing well to coat. Serve immediately.

Pasta Tubes with Meat and Cheese Sauce

The two sauces complement each other perfectly in this wonderfully flavoursome dish.

INGREDIENTS

Serves 4

350g/12oz rigatoni

salt and ground black pepper

fresh basil sprigs, to garnish

For the meat sauce

15ml/1 tbsp olive oil

350g/12oz/3 cups minced beef

1 onion, chopped

1 garlic clove, chopped

400g/14oz can chopped tomatoes

15ml/1 tbsp dried mixed herbs

30ml/2 tbsp tomato purée

For the cheese sauce

50g/2oz/¼ cup butter

50g/2oz/½ cup plain flour

450ml/¾ pint/1¾ cups milk

2 egg yolks

50g/2oz/½ cup freshly grated
  Parmesan cheese

1 To make the meat sauce, heat the oil in a large frying pan and fry the beef for 10 minutes, stirring occasionally until browned. Add the onion and cook for 5 minutes, stirring occasionally.

2 Stir in the garlic, tomatoes, herbs and tomato purée. Bring to the boil, cover, and simmer for about 30 minutes.

3 Meanwhile, to make the cheese sauce, melt the butter in a small saucepan, then stir in the flour and cook for 2 minutes, stirring constantly.

4 Remove the pan from the heat and gradually stir in the milk. Return the pan to the heat and bring to the boil, stirring occasionally, until thickened.

5 Add the egg yolks, cheese and seasoning and stir until the sauce is well blended.

6 Preheat the grill. Meanwhile, cook the pasta in plenty of boiling salted water according to the instructions on the packet. Drain thoroughly and turn into a large mixing bowl. Pour over the meat sauce and toss to coat.

7 Divide the pasta among four flameproof dishes. Spoon over the cheese sauce and place under the grill until brown. Serve immediately, garnished with fresh basil.

Linguine with Clams, Leeks and Tomatoes

Canned clams make this a speedy dish for those in a real hurry.

INGREDIENTS

Serves 4

350g/12oz linguine

25g/1oz/2 tbsp butter

2 leeks, thinly sliced

150ml/¼ pint/⅔ cup dry white wine

4 tomatoes, skinned, seeded and chopped

pinch of turmeric (optional)

250g/9oz can clams, drained

30ml/2 tbsp chopped fresh basil

60ml/4 tbsp crème fraîche

salt and ground black pepper

1 Cook the pasta in plenty of boiling salted water according to the instructions on the packet.

2 Meanwhile, melt the butter in a small saucepan and fry the sliced leeks for about 5 minutes until softened.

3 Add the wine, tomatoes and turmeric, bring to the boil and boil until reduced by half.

4 Stir in the clams, basil, crème fraîche and seasoning and heat through gently without boiling the sauce.

5 Drain the pasta thoroughly and toss in the clam and leek sauce. Serve immediately.

Macaroni with King Prawns and Ham

Cooked radicchio makes a novel addition to this sauce.

INGREDIENTS

Serves 4

350g/12oz short macaroni

45ml/3 tbsp olive oil

12 shelled raw king prawns

1 garlic clove, chopped

175g/6oz/generous 1 cup diced
    smoked ham

150ml/¼ pint/⅔ cup red wine

½ small radicchio lettuce, shredded

2 egg yolks, beaten

30ml/2 tbsp chopped fresh flat leaf parsley

150ml/¼ pint/⅔ cup double cream

salt and ground black pepper

shredded fresh basil, to garnish

1 Cook the pasta in plenty of boiling salted water, according to the instructions on the packet.

2 Meanwhile, heat the oil in a frying pan and cook the prawns, garlic and ham for about 5 minutes, stirring occasionally until the prawns are tender. Be careful not to overcook.

3 Add the wine and radicchio, bring to the boil and boil rapidly until the juices are reduced by about half.

4 Stir in the egg yolks, parsley and cream and bring almost to the boil, stirring constantly, then simmer until the sauce thickens slightly. Check the seasoning and adjust if necessary.

5 Drain the pasta thoroughly and toss in the sauce to coat. Serve immediately, garnished with some shredded fresh basil.

Penne with Aubergine and Mint Pesto

This splendid variation on the classic Italian pesto uses fresh mint rather than basil for a deliciously different flavour.

INGREDIENTS

Serves 4

2 large aubergines
450g/1lb penne
50g/2oz/½ cup walnut halves
salt and ground black pepper

For the pesto

25g/1oz fresh mint
15g/½oz flat leaf parsley
40g/1½oz/scant ½ cup walnuts
40g/1½oz finely grated Parmesan cheese
2 garlic cloves
90ml/6 tbsp olive oil

1 Cut the aubergines lengthways into 1cm/½in slices.

2 Cut the slices again crossways to give short strips.

3 Layer the strips in a colander with salt and leave to stand for 30 minutes over a plate to catch any juices. Rinse well in cool water and then drain thoroughly.

4 Place all the pesto ingredients, except the oil, in a blender or food processor. Blend until very smooth, then gradually add the oil in a thin stream until the mixture amalgamates. Season to taste.

5 Cook the penne in plenty of boiling salted water according to the instructions on the packet for about 8 minutes or until *al dente*. Add the aubergine and cook for a further 3 minutes.

6 Drain the pasta well and mix in the mint pesto and walnut halves. Serve immediately.

Chow Mein

One of the most well-known Chinese noodle dishes.

INGREDIENTS

Serves 4

225g/8oz Chinese egg noodles

30ml/2 tbsp oil

1 onion, chopped

1cm/½in piece fresh root ginger, chopped

2 garlic cloves, crushed

30ml/2 tbsp soy sauce

50ml/2fl oz/¼ cup dry white wine

10ml/2 tsp Chinese five-spice powder

450g/1lb/4 cups minced pork

4 spring onions, sliced

50g/2oz oyster mushrooms

75g/3oz bamboo shoots

15ml/1 tbsp sesame oil

prawn crackers, to serve

1 Cook the noodles in boiling water for 4 minutes and drain.

2 Meanwhile, heat the oil in a wok and add the onion, ginger, garlic, soy sauce and wine. Cook for 1 minute. Stir in the Chinese five-spice powder.

3 Add the minced pork and cook for 10 minutes, stirring constantly. Add the spring onions, oyster mushrooms and bamboo shoots and continue to cook for a further 5 minutes.

4 Stir in the noodles and sesame oil. Mix all the ingredients together well and serve at once with prawn crackers.

Macaroni Cheese with Mushrooms

Macaroni cheese is an all-time classic from the mid-week menu. Here it is served in a light creamy sauce with mushrooms and topped with pine nuts.

INGREDIENTS

Serves 4

450g/1lb quick-cooking elbow macaroni

45ml/3 tbsp olive oil

225g/8oz button mushrooms, sliced

2 fresh thyme sprigs

60ml/4 tbsp plain flour

1 vegetable stock cube

600ml/1 pint/2½ cups milk

2.5ml/½ tsp celery salt

5ml/1 tsp Dijon mustard

175g/6oz/1½ cups grated
    Cheddar cheese

25g/1oz/¼ cup freshly grated
    Parmesan cheese

25g/1oz/2 tbsp pine nuts

salt and ground black pepper

1 Cook the macaroni in plenty of boiling salted water according to the instructions on the packet.

COOK'S TIP

Closed button mushrooms are best for white cream sauces. Open varieties can darken a pale sauce to an unattractive sludgy grey.

---

2 Heat the oil in a heavy-based saucepan. Add the mushrooms and thyme, cover and cook over a gentle heat for 2–3 minutes. Stir in the flour and remove from the heat, add the stock cube and stir continuously until evenly blended. Add the milk, a little at a time, stirring after each addition. Add the celery salt, mustard and Cheddar cheese and season. Stir and simmer for 1–2 minutes until the sauce is thickened.

3 Preheat a moderate grill. Drain the macaroni; toss into the sauce. Turn into four individual dishes or one large flameproof gratin dish. Scatter with grated Parmesan cheese and pine nuts; grill until brown and bubbly.

Pasta with Roasted Vegetables

Sweet roasted vegetables form the basis of a rich sauce.

INGREDIENTS

Serves 4

1 large onion

1 aubergine

2 courgettes

2 peppers, preferably red or yellow, seeded

450g/1lb tomatoes, preferably plum

2–3 garlic cloves, coarsely chopped

60ml/4 tbsp olive oil

300ml/½ pint/1¼ cups smooth
    tomato sauce

50g/2oz black olives, stoned and halved

375–450g/12oz–1lb dried penne

salt and ground black pepper

15g/½oz fresh basil, shredded, to garnish

freshly grated Parmesan or pecorino
    cheese, to serve

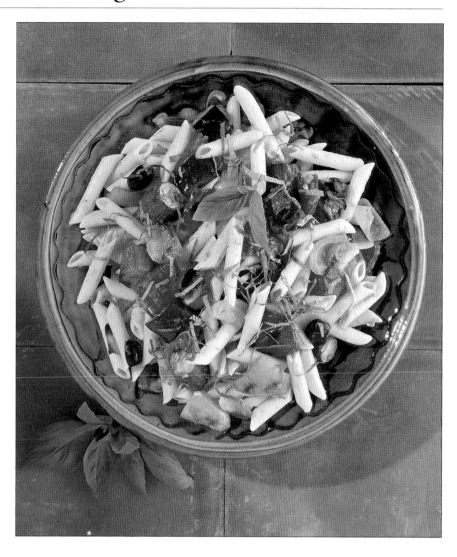

1 Preheat the oven to 240°C/ 475°F/Gas 9. Cut the onion, aubergine, courgettes, peppers and tomatoes into 2.5–4cm/1–1½in chunks. Scoop out and discard the tomato seeds.

2 Spread out the vegetables in a large roasting tin. Sprinkle the garlic and oil over the vegetables and stir and turn to mix evenly. Season with salt and pepper.

3 Roast the vegetables for about 30 minutes or until they are soft and browned (don't worry if the edges are charred black). Stir after 15 minutes.

4 Scrape the vegetable mixture into a saucepan. Add the tomato sauce and olives.

5 Cook the pasta in plenty of boiling salted water, according to the instructions on the packet, until *al dente.*

6 Meanwhile, heat the tomato and roasted vegetable sauce. Taste and adjust the seasoning if necessary.

7 Drain the pasta and return to the pan. Add the tomato and roasted vegetable sauce and stir to mix well. Serve hot, sprinkled with the basil. If you like, serve with freshly grated Parmesan or pecorino cheese handed separately.

Spaghetti with Mussels and Saffron

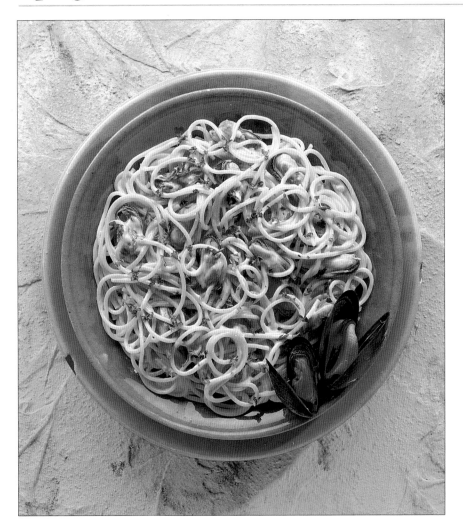

In this recipe the pasta is tossed with a delicious pale yellow mussel sauce, streaked with yellow strands of saffron. Powdered saffron will do just as well, but don't use turmeric – the flavour will be too strong.

INGREDIENTS

Serves 4

900g/2lb live mussels, in the shell

150ml/¼ pint/⅔ cup dry white wine

2 shallots, finely chopped

25g/1oz/2 tbsp butter

2 garlic cloves, crushed

10ml/2 tsp cornflour

300ml/½ pint/1¼ cups double cream

pinch of saffron strands

juice of ½ lemon

1 egg yolk

450g/1lb spaghetti

salt and ground black pepper

chopped fresh parsley, to garnish

1 Scrub the mussels and rinse well. Pull off any "beards" and leave the mussels to soak in cold water for 30 minutes. Tap each mussel sharply after this time. Discard any that do not close straightaway.

2 Drain the mussels and place in a large saucepan. Add the wine and shallots, cover and cook, shaking frequently, over a high heat for 5–10 minutes until the mussels are open. Discard any that do not open.

3 Drain the mussels through a sieve, reserving the liquid. Remove most of the mussels from their shells, reserving some in the shell to use as a garnish. Boil the reserved liquid rapidly until reduced by half.

4 Melt the butter in another saucepan, add the garlic and cook until golden. Stir in the cornflour and gradually stir in the cooking liquid and the cream. Add the saffron and seasoning and simmer until slightly thickened.

5 Stir in lemon juice to taste, then the egg yolk and mussels. Keep warm, but do not boil.

6 Cook the pasta according to the instructions on the packet. Drain. Toss the mussels with the spaghetti, top with the reserved mussels and sprinkle with the parsley. Serve with crusty bread, if you like.

Prawns with Tagliatelle in Packets

A quick and impressive dish, easy to prepare in advance and cook at the last minute. When the paper packets are opened at the table, the filling smells wonderful.

INGREDIENTS

Serves 4

750g/1¾lb raw prawns in the shell

450g/1lb tagliatelle or similar pasta

150ml/¼ pint/⅔ cup fresh or ready-made pesto sauce

20ml/4 tsp olive oil

1 garlic clove, crushed

120ml/4fl oz/½ cup dry white wine

salt and ground black pepper

1 Preheat the oven to 200°C/400°F/Gas 6. Twist the heads off the prawns and discard.

2 Cook the tagliatelle in plenty of rapidly boiling salted water for 2 minutes only, then drain. Mix with half the pesto.

3 Cut four 30cm/12in squares of greaseproof paper and place 5ml/1 tsp olive oil in the centre of each. Pile equal amounts of pasta in the middle of each square.

4 Top with equal amounts of prawns and spoon over the remaining pesto mixed with the garlic. Season with pepper; sprinkle each with the wine.

5 Brush the edges of the paper lightly with water and bring them loosely up around the filling, twisting to enclose. (The parcels should look like money bags.)

6 Place the parcels on a baking sheet. Bake in the oven for 10–15 minutes. Serve at once, allowing the diners to open their own packets at the table.

Coriander Ravioli with Pumpkin Filling

This stunning herb pasta is served with a superb creamy pumpkin and roast garlic filling.

INGREDIENTS

Serves 4–6

200g/7oz/scant 1 cup strong white flour

2 eggs

pinch of salt

45ml/3 tbsp chopped fresh coriander

coriander sprigs, to garnish

For the filling

4 garlic cloves, unpeeled

450g/1lb pumpkin, peeled and seeded

115g/4oz/½ cup ricotta cheese

4 sun-dried tomatoes in olive oil, drained
   and finely chopped, and
   30ml/2 tbsp of the oil

ground black pepper

1 Place the flour, eggs, salt and chopped fresh coriander into a blender or food processor and pulse until combined.

2 Place the dough on a lightly floured board and knead well for 5 minutes, until smooth. Wrap in clear film and leave to rest in the fridge for 20 minutes.

3 Preheat the oven to 200°C/400°F/Gas 6. Place the garlic cloves on a baking sheet and bake for 10 minutes until soft. Steam the pumpkin for 5–8 minutes until tender and drain well. Peel the garlic cloves and mash into the pumpkin together with the ricotta cheese and drained sun-dried tomatoes. Season with lots of ground black pepper.

4 Divide the pasta into four pieces and flatten slightly. Using a pasta machine, on its thinnest setting, roll out each piece. Leave the sheets of pasta on a clean dish towel until they are slightly dried.

5 Using a 7.5cm/3in crinkle-edged round cutter, stamp out 36 rounds of pasta.

6 Top 18 of the rounds with a teaspoonful of filling, brush the edges with water and place another round of pasta on top. Press firmly around the edges to seal. Bring a large pan of water to the boil, add the ravioli and cook for 3–4 minutes. Drain well and toss into the reserved tomato oil. Serve at once garnished with fresh coriander sprigs.

Pasta with Low-fat Pesto Sauce

Traditionally made with lashings of olive oil, this simple pesto sauce is still packed with flavour.

INGREDIENTS

Serves 4

225g/8oz dried pasta, such as spirals

50g/2oz/1 cup fresh basil leaves

25g/1oz/½ cup parsley sprigs

1 garlic clove, crushed

25g/1oz/¼ cup pine nuts

115g/4oz/½ cup curd cheese

30ml/2 tbsp freshly grated Parmesan cheese

salt and ground black pepper

fresh basil sprigs, to garnish

1 Cook the pasta in plenty of boiling salted water in a large saucepan for 8–10 minutes, or until *al dente*. Drain well.

2 Meanwhile put half the basil and half the parsley, the garlic clove, pine nuts and curd cheese into a blender or food processor fitted with a metal blade and process until smooth.

3 Add the remaining basil and parsley together with the Parmesan cheese and seasoning. Continue to process until the herbs are finely chopped.

4 Toss the pasta with the pesto and serve on warmed plates. Garnish with fresh basil sprigs.

Spinach and Hazelnut Lasagne

*A vegetarian dish which is hearty
enough to satisfy meat-eaters too.
Use frozen spinach – you will need
450g/1lb – if you're short of time.*

INGREDIENTS

Serves 4

900g/2lb fresh spinach

300ml/½ pint/1¼ cups vegetable or
   chicken stock

1 onion, finely chopped

1 garlic clove, crushed

75g/3oz/¾ cup hazelnuts

30ml/2 tbsp chopped fresh basil

6 lasagne sheets

400g/14oz can chopped tomatoes

200g/7oz/scant 1 cup low-fat fromage frais

flaked hazelnuts and chopped parsley,
   to garnish

1 Preheat the oven to 200°C/
400°F/Gas 6. Wash the fresh
spinach and place in a pan with
just the water that clings to the
leaves. Cook the spinach over a
fairly high heat for 2 minutes until
wilted. Drain well.

2 Heat 30ml/2 tbsp of the stock
in a large pan and simmer the
onion and garlic until soft. Stir in
the spinach, hazelnuts and basil.

3 In a large ovenproof dish, layer
the spinach, lasagne and the
tomatoes. Season well between the
layers. Pour over the remaining
stock. Spread the low-fat fromage
frais over the top.

4 Bake the lasagne for about
45 minutes, or until golden
brown. Serve hot, sprinkled with
lines of flaked hazelnuts and
chopped parsley.

Tagliatelle with Gorgonzola Sauce

Gorgonzola is a creamy Italian blue cheese. As an alternative you could use Danish Blue or Pipo Creme.

INGREDIENTS

Serves 4

25g/1oz/2 tbsp butter, plus extra for
    tossing the pasta
225g/8oz Gorgonzola cheese
150ml/¼ pint/⅔ cup double or
    whipping cream
30ml/2 tbsp dry vermouth
5ml/1 tsp cornflour
15ml/1 tbsp chopped fresh sage
450g/1lb tagliatelle
salt and ground black pepper

1 Melt 25g/1oz/2 tbsp butter in a heavy saucepan (it needs to be thick-based to prevent the cheese from burning). Stir in 175g/6oz crumbled Gorgonzola cheese and stir over a gentle heat for about 2–3 minutes until melted.

2 Whisk in the cream, vermouth and cornflour. Add the sage; season. Cook, whisking, until the sauce boils and thickens. Set aside.

3 Boil the pasta in plenty of salted water according to the instructions on the packet. Drain well and toss with a little butter.

4 Reheat the sauce gently, whisking well. Divide the pasta among four serving bowls, top with the sauce and sprinkle over the remaining crumbled cheese. Serve immediately.

Pasta with Tomato and Cream Sauce

Here pasta is served with a deliciously rich version of an ordinary tomato sauce.

INGREDIENTS

Serves 4–6

30ml/2 tbsp olive oil

2 garlic cloves, crushed

400g/14oz can chopped tomatoes

150ml/¼ pint/⅔ cup double or
   whipping cream

30ml/2 tbsp chopped fresh herbs, such as
   basil, oregano or parsley

450g/1lb pasta, any variety

salt and ground black pepper

1 Heat the oil in a medium saucepan, add the garlic and cook for 2 minutes, until golden.

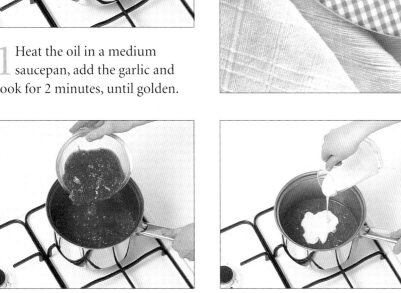

2 Stir in the tomatoes, bring to the boil and simmer uncovered for 20 minutes, stirring occasionally to prevent sticking. The sauce is ready when you can see the oil separating on top.

3 Add the cream, bring slowly to the boil again and simmer until slightly thickened. Stir in the herbs, taste and season well.

4 Cook the pasta in plenty of boiling salted water according to the instructions on the packet. Drain well and toss with the sauce. Serve piping hot, sprinkled with extra herbs, if you like.

PASTA
SAUCES

Ravioli with Four-cheese Sauce

This is a smooth, cheesy sauce that coats the pasta very evenly.

INGREDIENTS

Serves 4

350g/12oz ravioli
50g/2oz/¼ cup butter
50g/2oz/¼ cup plain flour
450ml/¾ pint/1¾ cups milk
50g/2oz Parmesan cheese
50g/2oz Edam cheese
50g/2oz Gruyère cheese
50g/2oz fontina cheese
salt and ground black pepper
chopped fresh flat leaf parsley, to garnish

1 Cook the pasta in plenty of boiling salted water according to the instructions on the packet.

2 Melt the butter in a saucepan, stir in the flour and cook for 2 minutes, stirring occasionally.

3 Gradually stir in the milk until completely blended.

4 Bring the milk slowly to the boil, stirring constantly until the sauce is thickened.

5 Grate the cheeses and stir them into the sauce. Stir until they are just beginning to melt. Remove from the heat and season.

6 Drain the pasta thoroughly and turn into a large serving dish. Pour over the sauce and toss to coat. Serve immediately, garnished with the chopped fresh parsley.

Spaghetti in a Cream and Bacon Sauce

This is a light and creamy sauce flavoured with bacon and lightly cooked eggs.

INGREDIENTS

Serves 4

350g/12oz spaghetti

15ml/1 tbsp olive oil

1 onion, chopped

115g/4oz rindless streaky bacon or
  pancetta, diced

1 garlic clove, chopped

3 eggs

300ml/½ pint/1¼ cups double cream

50g/2oz Parmesan cheese

chopped fresh basil, to garnish

1 Cook the pasta in plenty of boiling salted water according to the instructions on the packet.

2 Heat the oil in a frying pan and fry the onion and bacon or pancetta for 10 minutes, until softened. Stir in the garlic and fry for a further 2 minutes, stirring occasionally.

3 Meanwhile, beat the eggs in a bowl, then stir in the cream and seasoning. Grate the Parmesan cheese and stir into the egg and cream mixture.

4 Stir the cream mixture into the onion and bacon or pancetta and cook over a low heat for a few minutes, stirring constantly, until heated through. Season to taste.

5 Drain the pasta thoroughly and turn into a large serving dish. Pour over the sauce and toss to coat. Serve immediately, garnished with chopped fresh basil.

Pasta Twists with Cream and Cheese

Soured cream and two cheeses make a lovely rich sauce.

INGREDIENTS

Serves 4

350g/12oz pasta twists, such as spirali

25g/1oz/2 tbsp butter

1 onion, chopped

1 garlic clove, chopped

15ml/1 tbsp chopped fresh oregano

300ml/½ pint/1¼ cups soured cream

75g/3oz/¾ cup grated mozzarella cheese

75g/3oz/¾ cup grated Bel Paese cheese

5 sun-dried tomatoes in oil, drained
   and sliced

salt and ground black pepper

1 Cook the pasta in plenty of boiling salted water according to the instructions on the packet.

2 Melt the butter in a large frying pan and fry the onion for about 10 minutes until softened. Add the garlic and cook for 1 minute.

3 Stir in the oregano and cream and heat gently until almost boiling. Stir in the mozzarella and Bel Paese cheese and heat gently, stirring occasionally, until melted. Add the sun-dried tomatoes and season to taste.

4 Drain the pasta twists well and turn into a serving dish. Pour over the sauce and toss well to coat. Serve immediately.

Cannelloni with Cheese and Coriander

A speedy supper dish, this is best served with a simple tomato and fresh basil salad.

INGREDIENTS

Serves 4

450g/1lb cannelloni

115g/4oz full-fat garlic-and-herb cheese

30ml/2 tbsp very finely chopped
   fresh coriander

300ml/½ pint/1¼ cups single cream

115g/4oz/1 cup shelled peas, cooked

salt and ground black pepper

1 Cook the pasta in plenty of boiling salted water according to the instructions on the packet.

2 Melt the cheese in a small pan over a low heat until smooth.

3 Stir in the coriander, cream and salt and pepper. Bring slowly to the boil, stirring occasionally, until well blended. Stir in the peas and continue cooking until heated through.

4 Drain the pasta and turn into a large serving dish. Pour over the sauce and toss well to coat thoroughly. Serve immediately.

COOK'S TIP

If you do not like the pronounced flavour of fresh coriander, substitute another fresh herb, such as basil or flat leaf parsley.

Basic Tomato Sauce

Tomato sauce is without doubt the most popular dressing for pasta in Italy. This sauce is best made with fresh tomatoes, but works well with canned plum tomatoes.

INGREDIENTS

Serves 4

60ml/4 tbsp olive oil

1 onion, very finely chopped

1 garlic clove, finely chopped

450g/1lb tomatoes, fresh or canned, chopped with their juice

a few fresh basil leaves or parsley sprigs

salt and ground black pepper

1 Heat the oil in a medium saucepan. Add the onion, and cook over a moderate heat until it is translucent, 5–8 minutes.

2 Stir in the garlic and the tomatoes with their juice (add 45ml/3 tbsp of water if you are using fresh tomatoes). Season with salt and pepper. Add the herbs. Cook for 20–30 minutes.

3 Pass the sauce through a food mill or purée in a blender or food processor. To serve, reheat gently, correct the seasoning and pour over drained pasta.

Special Tomato Sauce

The tomatoes in this sauce are enhanced by the addition of extra vegetables. It is good served with all types of pasta.

INGREDIENTS

Serves 6

700g/1⅔lb tomatoes, fresh or canned, chopped

1 carrot, chopped

1 celery stick, chopped

1 onion, chopped

1 garlic clove, crushed

75ml/5 tbsp olive oil

a few fresh basil leaves or small pinch dried oregano

salt and ground black pepper

1 Place all the ingredients in a medium heavy saucepan, and simmer for 30 minutes.

2 Purée the sauce in a blender or food processor; alternatively press through a sieve.

3 Return the sauce to the pan, correct the seasoning, and bring to a simmer. Cook for about 15 minutes, then pour over drained cooked pasta.

COOK'S TIP

This sauce may be spooned into freezer bags and frozen until required. Allow to thaw at room temperature before reheating.

Fusilli with Mascarpone and Spinach

This creamy, green sauce tossed in lightly cooked pasta is best served with plenty of sun-dried tomato ciabatta bread.

INGREDIENTS

Serves 4

350g/12oz pasta spirals, such as fusilli

50g/2oz/¼ cup butter

1 onion, chopped

1 garlic clove, chopped

30ml/2 tbsp fresh thyme leaves

225g/8oz frozen spinach leaves, thawed

225g/8oz/1 cup mascarpone cheese

salt and ground black pepper

fresh thyme sprigs, to garnish

1 Cook the pasta in plenty of boiling salted water according to the instructions on the packet.

2 Melt the butter in a large saucepan and fry the onion for 10 minutes until softened.

3 Stir in the garlic, fresh thyme, spinach and seasoning and heat gently for about 5 minutes, stirring occasionally, until heated through.

4 Stir in the mascarpone cheese and cook gently until heated through. Do not boil.

5 Drain the pasta thoroughly and stir into the sauce. Toss until well coated. Serve immediately, garnished with fresh thyme.

COOK'S TIP

Mascarpone is a rich Italian cream cheese. If you cannot find any, use ordinary full-fat cream cheese instead.

Spaghetti with Mixed Mushrooms

This combination of mixed mushrooms and freshly chopped sweet basil tossed with spaghetti would be well complemented by a simple tomato salad.

Serves 4

50g/2oz/¼ cup butter

1 onion, chopped

350g/12oz spaghetti

350g/12oz mixed mushrooms, such as
    brown, flat and button, sliced

1 garlic clove, chopped

300ml/½ pint/1¼ cups soured cream

30ml/2 tbsp chopped fresh basil

50g/2oz/½ cup freshly grated
    Parmesan cheese

salt and ground black pepper

torn flat leaf parsley, to garnish

freshly grated Parmesan cheese, to serve

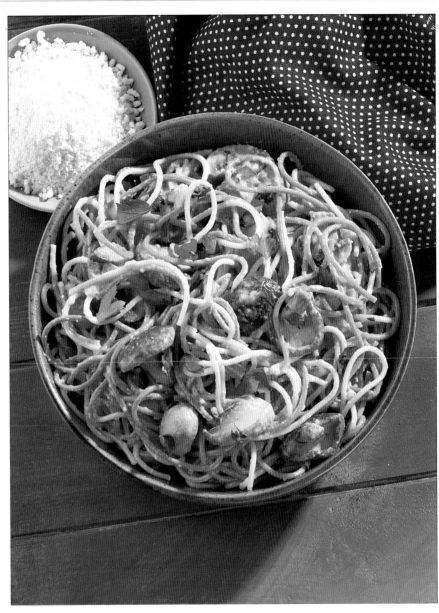

1 Melt the butter in a large frying pan and fry the chopped onion for 10 minutes until softened.

2 Cook the pasta in plenty of boiling salted water according to the instructions on the packet.

3 Stir the mushrooms and garlic into the onion mixture and fry for 10 minutes until softened.

4 Add the soured cream, basil, grated Parmesan cheese and salt and pepper to taste. Cover and heat through.

5 Drain the pasta thoroughly and toss with the sauce. Serve immediately, garnished with torn flat leaf parsley, with plenty of grated Parmesan cheese.

Curly Lasagne with Classic Tomato Sauce

A classic sauce that is simply delicious just served by itself.

INGREDIENTS

Serves 4

30ml/2 tbsp olive oil

1 onion, chopped

30ml/2 tbsp tomato purée

5ml/1 tsp paprika

2 × 400g/14oz cans chopped
  tomatoes, drained

pinch of dried oregano

300ml/½ pint/1¼ cups dry red wine

large pinch of caster sugar

350g/12oz curly lasagne

salt and ground black pepper

Parmesan cheese shavings, to serve

chopped fresh flat leaf parsley, to garnish

1 Heat the oil in a large frying pan and fry the onion for 10 minutes, stirring occasionally, until softened. Add the tomato purée and paprika and cook for a further 3 minutes.

2 Add the tomatoes, oregano, wine and sugar and season to taste, then bring to the boil.

3 Simmer for 20 minutes until the sauce has reduced and thickened, stirring occasionally.

4 Meanwhile, cook the pasta in plenty of boiling salted water according to the instructions on the packet. Drain thoroughly and turn into a large serving dish. Pour over the sauce and toss to coat. Serve sprinkled with Parmesan cheese shavings and the chopped fresh flat leaf parsley.

COOK'S TIP

If you cannot find curly lasasgne use plain lasagne snipped in half lengthways.

Pasta Spirals with Pesto Sauce

A light, fragrant sauce like this dish gives a temptingly different taste.

INGREDIENTS

Serves 4

350g/12oz pasta spirals (fusilli)

50g/2oz fresh basil leaves, without the stalks

2 garlic cloves, chopped

30ml/2 tbsp pine nuts

salt and freshly ground black pepper

150ml/¼ pint/⅔ cup olive oil

50g/2oz/⅓ cup Parmesan cheese, freshly grated, plus extra to garnish

fresh basil sprigs, to garnish

COOK'S TIP

Fresh basil is widely available from most greengrocers and supermarkets, either in growing pots or packets. If you buy a plant, remove the flowers as they appear so the plant grows more leaves.

Pesto is best kept in a screw-topped jar in the fridge for up to two days. If you want to keep it a few days longer, cover the top with a thin layer of olive oil. This can be stirred into the sauce when you are ready to add it to hot pasta.

---

1 Cook the pasta following the instructions on the packet until *al dente*.

2 To make the pesto sauce, place the basil leaves, garlic, pine nuts, seasoning and olive oil in a food processor or blender. Blend until very creamy.

3 Transfer the mixture to a bowl and stir in the freshly grated Parmesan cheese.

4 Drain the pasta thoroughly and turn it into a large bowl. Pour the sauce over and toss to coat. Divide among serving plates and serve, sprinkled with the extra Parmesan cheese and garnished with fresh basil sprigs.

Pasta Twists with Classic Meat Sauce

This is a rich meat sauce which is ideal to serve with all types of pasta. The sauce definitely improves if kept overnight in the fridge. This allows the flavours time to mature.

INGREDIENTS

Serves 4

450g/1lb/4 cups minced beef

115g/4oz smoked streaky beacon, rinded and chopped

1 onion, chopped

2 celery sticks, chopped

15ml/1 tbsp plain flour

150ml/¼ pint/⅔ cup chicken stock or water

45ml/3 tbsp tomato purée

1 garlic clove, chopped

45ml/3 tbsp chopped fresh mixed herbs, such as oregano, parsley, marjoram and chives or 15ml/1 tbsp dried mixed herbs

15ml/1 tbsp redcurrant jelly

350g/12oz pasta twists, such as spirali

salt and ground black pepper

chopped oregano, to garnish

1 Heat a large saucepan and fry the beef and bacon for about 10 minutes, stirring occasionally until browned.

2 Add the chopped onion and celery and cook for 2 minutes, stirring occasionally.

3 Stir in the flour and cook for 2 minutes, stirring constantly.

4 Pour in the stock or water and bring to the boil.

5 Stir in the tomato purée, garlic, herbs, redcurrant jelly and seasoning. Bring to the boil, cover and simmer for about 30 minutes.

6 Cook the pasta in plenty of boiling salted water according to the instructions on the packet. Drain thoroughly and turn into a large serving dish. Pour over the sauce and toss to coat. Serve the pasta immediately, garnished with chopped fresh oregano.

COOK'S TIP

The redcurrant jelly helps to draw out the flavour of the tomato purée. You can use a sweet mint jelly or chutney instead, if you like

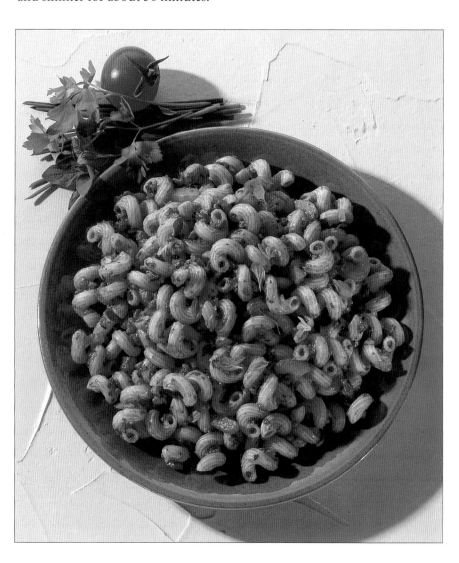

Macaroni with Hazelnut and Coriander Sauce

This is a variation on pesto sauce, giving a smooth, herby flavour of coriander.

INGREDIENTS

Serves 4

350g/12oz macaroni

50g/2oz/⅓ cup hazelnuts

2 garlic cloves

1 bunch fresh coriander

1 tsp salt

90ml/6 tbsp olive oil

fresh coriander sprigs, to garnish

1 Cook the pasta following the instructions on the packet, until *al dente*.

2 Meanwhile, finely chop the hazelnuts.

COOK'S TIP

To remove the skins from the hazelnuts, place them in a 180°C/350°F/Gas 4 oven for 20 minutes, then rub off the skins with a clean dish towel.

3 Place the nuts and remaining ingredients, except 1 tbsp of the oil, in a food processor, or use a pestle and mortar and grind together to create the sauce.

4 Heat the remaining oil in a saucepan and add the sauce. Fry very gently for about 1 minute until heated through.

5 Drain the pasta thoroughly and stir it into the sauce. Toss well to coat. Serve immediately, garnished with fresh coriander.

Spaghetti with Bacon and Tomato Sauce

This substantial sauce is a meal in itself, so serve it up as a warming winter supper.

INGREDIENTS

Serves 4

15ml/1 tbsp olive oil

225g/8oz smoked streaky bacon, rinded and roughly chopped

250g/9oz spaghetti

5ml/1 tsp chilli powder

1 quantity Classic Tomato Sauce (see Curly Lasagne with Classic Tomato Sauce)

salt and ground black pepper

roughly chopped fresh flat leaf parsley, to garnish

1 Heat the oil in large frying pan and fry the bacon for about 10 minutes, stirring occasionally until crisp and golden.

2 Cook the pasta following the instructions on the packet, until *al dente*.

3 Add the chilli powder to the bacon and cook for 2 minutes. Stir in the tomato sauce and bring to the boil. Cover and simmer for 10 minutes. Season with salt and pepper to taste.

4 Drain the pasta thoroughly and toss it together with the sauce. Serve garnished with the roughly chopped fresh parsley.

Tagliattelle with Pea and Ham Sauce

A colourful sauce, this is ideal served with crusty Italian or French bread.

INGREDIENTS

Serves 4

350g/12oz tagliatelle

225g/8oz/1½ cups shelled peas

300ml/½ pint/1¼ cups single cream

50g/2oz/⅓ cup freshly grated fontina cheese

75g/3oz Parma ham, sliced into strips

salt and ground black pepper

1 Cook the pasta following the instructions on the packet until *al dente*.

2 Plunge the peas into a pan of boiling salted water and cook for about 7 minutes or until tender. Drain and set aside.

3 Place the cream and half the fontina cheese in a small saucepan and heat gently, stirring constantly until heated through.

4 Drain the pasta thoroughly and turn it into a large serving bowl. Toss together the pasta, ham and peas and pour on the sauce. Add the remaining cheese and season with salt and pepper to taste.

Index